DOES WHICH BIBLE REALLY MATTER ?

davereese6@msn.com

www.right-division.com

PO Box 4574

Beeville, Texas 78104

INTRODUCTION

Some King James Bible critics invented the term "King James Version Onlyist" to cast aspersion on those who believe the KJB is an inerrant English translation of scripture. The implication of "Onlyist" is that any person who believes the KJB is an accurate English translation of scripture is uneducated and ignorant of translation and language facts. Nothing could be further from the truth.

Throwing charges of "KJV onlyist" and "Originals ONLY" back and forth accomplish nothing but entertainment for the choir — rather, serious answers to specific charges of error on both sides of the aisle is beneficial. Scholarship (however defined plus ignorance) exists in KJV and critic camps.

KJV critics do not hold a monopoly on education. Many of those who believe in the superiority and infallibility of the King James Bible hold undergraduate and post graduate degrees.

The education of King James Bible critics and believers is not questioned. The issue lies deeper than education.

The author majored in English, Bible, and psychology in two colleges and holds two earned doctorates from seminary study. Like many educated idiots, I did not believe the KJB was accurate upon graduation. Years ago, I believed the King James Version was a *reliable* translation but not entirely accurate or infallible and certainly not inspired. My seminary education taught that only the original manuscripts were inspired and that all translations had errors. *But we were to be encouraged* because scholars were seeking the best manuscripts and surely one day, we would have the best available. Seminary education did not study manuscript evidence, (the footnote apparatus in Nestle Greek grammar) nor did it address the issue of over 5000 extant Greek manuscripts, fragments, and copies. Our time was spent translating Bible books and memorizing mood, tense, and voice of Greek verbs and participles, wearing out the seat of our pants and paying dollars to learn why an inspired Bible was not extant.

After several years of personal study and burning the midnight oil I came out of the Bible fog in 1973. Simultaneous to manuscript and textual study was my notice that the translation of the Bible had become a profitable business, pulling in over a billion dollars a year in sales by the 1970s. Initially, every new translation carried the merchandising ploy that it was supposed to be an improvement over the preceding one: The RV of 1884 was good but the ASV of 1901 was better, the RSV of 1950 was even better, etc.,etc. When the "newest is the best" campaign fizzled out, specialized Bibles took over—the market soon featured "Youth Bible" "Ladies Bible" "Study Bible" "Teen Bible" "Senior Bible" – "New International Version" and "Christian Standard Bible" …well, you get the picture.

One seminary professor of my acquaintance had the highest scores ever made at Stetson University and earned a ThD degree from Louisville Baptist Theological Seminary. Dr. Aubrey Martin was 100% blind and memorized the entire 1901 American Standard Version NT. Dr. Martin accompanied Dr. William R. Newell on his nationwide Bible conference tours and shared speaking duties in the 1950s with him. Dr. Newell used only the ASV 1901 and authored commentaries: Romans, Hebrews, Revelation, etc. Dr. Martin's personal testimony was that he wished he had memorized the King James Version because it was superior to the ASV of 1901. Another educated KJB believer I knew was Dr. Philip Marquart, a Harvard Medical School graduate surgeon and psychiatrist. Dr. Dennis Spackman, a New Zealand MD surgeon, and zealous KJB believer was a close friend. These men I personally knew, are now with the Lord, and many other educated men and women can be cited.

I realize that post graduate degrees are not necessary to believing or understanding the KJB. Grandma on the front porch rocker can get more out of her KJB than many college professors.

No serious King James Bible believer holds that inerrant scripture is only found in the KJB or that all of the King James Bible's words are necessary for salvation—a gospel tract does not contain all of the Bible's words. All Bible versions in all languages contain at least *some* inerrant scripture words and verses. Competent believers hold that the Roman Catholic Bible in Latin contains some inerrant and inspired words. Even the New World Translation—the Jehovah Witness translation—contains some of the word of God

It is a different level of argument to claim there are no _proven_ errors in the KJB from the statement _"there are no errors"_ in the King James Version.

Reasonable men know that if you claim there are errors in a document, you must demonstrate your claim validity by identifying the specific errors and also correcting those errors—thereby producing an inerrant document. It is very easy to make a general claim of King James Bible errors without specificity, but another altogether to identify and correct the supposed errors. A man who claims some statement is in error but is unwilling or cannot identify and correct the error—thereby producing an inerrant statement, is reckoned to be mentally deficient or a liar.

The use of synonyms does not prevent inerrancy, inspiration, and infallibility of scripture. None of the three scripture values above depend upon the orthography or spelling of a word. A "deer" may also be spelled "deere"—that is no problem. It is a problem when the descriptive context of a subject proves the word to be erroneous. Whether the synonymous "hare" or "rabbit" is used is not an issue –it is when the near contextual statement is made "A hare weighs a minimum of 250 pounds and is carnivorous" that the issue of inerrancy arises. Or, when Genesis 1:1 is translated "In the beginning the gods created the heaven and the earth." The remote Bible context of monotheism and Trinitarianism in the KJB demands that "Elohim" (a plural number in Hebrew) be translated in Genesis 1 by the singular number in English, God.

Contrary to the general but faulty knowledge of 16th-17th century English language, the KJV translators of 1611 were exceptional grammarian wordsmiths. The ability of 16th to 17th century English language to give a definitive meaning to a word is unmatched in any language, including Greek.

The critics problem is not that they believe the King James Bible is full of errors. Their problem is that they DO NOT BELIEVE **ANY** MANUSCRIPT, BIBLE, OR TRANSLATION IN **ANY** LANGUAGE IS INERRANT OR INSPIRED !

DOES WHICH BIBLE REALLY MATTER?

The Greek word "marturo" is the etymological source of our English word, martyr. The Greek word carries the meaning of "witness" "testify" "testimony" "evidence" "proof" or "record". The KJB translates marturo as "witness" in John 5:31. The Bible states in its remote context that a single witness is not accepted as proof or evidence under Hebrew law; two or three witnesses that agree are accepted as proof (Deuteronomy 19:15). Examine "marturo" in John 5:31 and John 8:14.

John 5:31 <u>**If I bear witness**</u> **(marturo)** <u>**of myself**</u>**, my witness (marturo) is not true. (KJB)**

John 8:14 **Jesus answered and said unto them, Though** <u>**I bear record**</u> **(marturo)** <u>**of myself,**</u> *yet* <u>**my record**</u> **(marturo)** <u>**is true:**</u> **for I know whence I came, and whither I go; but ye cannot tell whence I come, and whither I go. (KJB)**

The KJB, following the Bible context, translates "marturo" as "witness" (a single testimony) in John 5:31. In other words, a single testimony is not acceptable as truth or as proof. But in John 8:14 the same Greek word "marturo" is translated "record" — which is an account of several singular witnesses or proofs. If "marturo" is not translated properly, error is in the translation.

<u>Both versions of John 5:31 in the New International Version and the Christian Standard Bible are correct and inerrant:</u>

John 5:31 "If I testify (marturo) about myself, my testimony (marturo) is not true." (NIV)
John 5:31 "If I testify (marturo) about myself, my testimony (marturo) is not true." (CSB)
<u>But watch how both fail inerrancy when the Biblical context of "marturo" is ignored in John 8:14:</u>

John 8:14 "Jesus answered, "Even if I testify (marturo) on my own behalf, my testimony (marturo) is valid, for I know where I came from and where I am going. But you have no idea where I come from or where I am going." (NIV)
John 8:14 "Even if I testify (marturo) about myself," Jesus replied, "My testimony (marturo) is true, because I know where I came from and where I'm going. But you don't know where I come from or where I'm going." (CSB)

The New International Version and the Christian Standard Bible both commit the same translation blunder and are not accurate in John 8:14. Both versions deny themselves and make the Lord Jesus Christ inconsistent in His words

This example demonstrates the flexibility of English and its ability to accurately take the context's determinate meaning of a word far beyond its surface or general meaning.

PROPHETS OR PROPHET ?

Mark 1:2 As it is written in the prophets, Behold, I send my messenger before thy face, which shall prepare thy way before thee. (KJB)

Mark 1:3 The voice of one crying in the wilderness, Prepare ye the way of the Lord, make his paths straight. (KJB)

Notice the King James Bible has plural "prophets". Both the New International Version and the Christian Standard Bible claim the quote is only from Isaiah the prophet:

"as it is written in Isaiah the prophet: "I will send my messenger ahead of you, who will prepare your way" (Mark 1:2 New International Version)

"a voice of one calling in the wilderness, 'Prepare the way for the Lord, make straight paths for him. (Mark 1:3 New International Version)

"As it is written in Isaiah the prophet: See, I am sending my messenger ahead of you;

he will prepare your way" (Mark 1:2 Christian Standard Bible)

"A voice of one crying out in the wilderness:

Prepare the way for the Lord; make his paths straight! (Mark 1:3 Christian Standard Bible)

Both the NIV and CSB (also RSV, ASV, NASB) claim the quote "I will send my messenger…" "I am sending my messenger…" is from Isaiah the prophet. In both the NIV and CSB Old Testament book of Isaiah the prophecy cannot be found!

Verse 3 in both the NIV and CSB claim Isaiah the prophet said: " A voice of one calling…" "A voice of one crying…". The book of Isaiah *does record that prophecy* but where do you find the prophecy "I will send my messenger…" in Isaiah? Answer: The prophecy is not there!

Where do you find both prophecies in the word of God? It takes two OT prophets. Answer: Isaiah and Malachi, just as the accurate KJB translation says: "the prophets".

COVENANT AND TESTAMENT DISTINCTIONS

"Diatheke" is the Greek word translated as "covenant" and "testament" in the KJB. The New International Version produces translation errors by translating diatheke as "covenant" and "will" but never by "testament". *The only place you will find "testament" in the NIV is in the list of "Old Testament" and "New Testament" books in the Table of Contents. "Testament" is not in the NIV translation text.*

The KJB exhibits the guidance of God in the translation of the Greek term (diatheke) by either "testament" or "covenant". When reading the KJB, there is no confusion between the Body of Christ's testament blessings and Israel's covenant promises, benefits, and blessings from the several covenants and the two testaments. In the KJB's translation of the Greek diatheke by both terms, the Body of Christ's blessings are from the New Testament with no promised covenants. There is no "New Covenant" made with the Body of Christ; the New Covenant is promised to a future generation of the nation of Israel. This is but one more proof of the AV1611 translators' finished product being more accurate than an individual or group effort.

There is a Biblical rule of context regarding covenants and the Body of Christ: Doctrinally, in the Old Testament, individuals and the nation of Israel, alone, were given covenants of promise; no covenant is made with the Body of Christ. Ephesians 2:12-13 makes it clear those in Christ Jesus were aliens from the nation of Israel, and never given covenant promises, but were brought nigh to God by the blood of the New Testament.

"That at that time ye were without Christ, being aliens from the commonwealth of Israel, and strangers from the covenants of promise, having no hope, and without God in the world: 13 But now in Christ Jesus ye who sometimes were far off are made nigh by the blood of Christ." (Ephesians 2:12-13 KJB)

The NIV even recognizes this truth:
"remember that at that time you were separate from Christ, excluded from citizenship in Israel and foreigners to the covenants of the promise, without hope and without God in the world. 13 But now in Christ Jesus you who once were far away have been brought near by the blood of Christ." (Ephesians 2:12-13 NIV)

But then the NIV confuses doctrine by stating that blood of the New Testament is the "blood of the covenant"!

"This is my blood of the covenant, which is poured out for many for the forgiveness of sins." (Matthew 26:28 NIV)

*"Testament" and "Covenant" are not synonymous.
All Deity Covenants are dependent upon
the fulfillment of the New Testament
Blood and Death and Resurrection of the Testator:
Jesus Christ.
The King James Bible translates
one Greek word (diatheke) as "testament" and "covenant"
by rule of contextual authority, thus avoiding the confusion
between "New Testament" and "New
Covenant" definitions caused
by the practice of uniform translation
found in most modern translations.*

The Body of Christ composed of both Jew and Gentile in one spiritual Body (a spiritual organism, not a physical organization or nation) is never given a covenant of promise.

The New International Version continues to confuse the distinction between a testament and a covenant and introduces a term "will" that adds to the errors of the NIV translation.

**16 "In the case of a will, it is necessary to prove the death of the one who made it,
17 because a will is in force only when somebody has died; it never takes effect while the one who made it is living.
18 This is why even the first covenant was not put into effect without blood." (Hebrews 9:16-18 New International Version)**

Introducing "a will" as translation of diatheke adds another problem to the NIV. "Will" dates the NIV as being out-of-date! As of 2022, a "will" no longer is "in force" upon the death of a person. Modern legal terms require an Estate Executer to control death benefits; a will only specifies final desire while the person is living. The NIV, by the inclusion of "will" apparently was an attempt to avoid the further translation problem of making all Bible "covenants" require death: *a covenant may but does not always require blood or death — see Genesis 9;21:32.*

It is true that diatheke *in Greek* carries any one of these meanings: disposition, contract, will, covenant, or testament. Any one of those general words, disposition, contract, will, or covenant may generally translate diatheke — but it is not true that any of those are permissible or accurate translations from the Biblical context. It is *not* proper English usage, nor is it within the Bible context of a "will" to make the NIV's claim, "…a will is in force only when somebody has died…"

The KJB sets the contextual definition of when a diatheke (translated only as testament) is in force:

"For where a testament is, there must also of necessity be the death of the testator." (Hebrews 9:16 KJB)

According to the KJB, a testament (diatheke) requires death; a covenant (diatheke) does not require death and this distinction is in perfect doctrinal harmony with the overall Biblical usage Thus, there is a clear and definitive difference between a testament and covenant proven by Biblical context. The NIV does nothing but confuse the reader on the meaning of testament and covenant and demonstrates the NIV translation errors.

LOVE AND CHARITY

"If I speak in the tongues of men or of angels, but do not have love, I am only a resounding gong or a clanging cymbal." (I Corinthians 13:1 New International Version) "If I speak in the tongues of men or of angels, but do not have love, I am only a resounding gong or a clanging cymbal." (1 Corinthians 13:1 Christian Standard Bible)

Bible translation does not only require proper translation of individual words, contextual usage of a word's meaning must also be considered and employed. The Greek word (agape) is translated "love" in 1 Corinthians 13:1 and in many cases in many versions. This general translation is not altogether wrong, but "love" is inadequate to the specific and definitive meaning of the agape context in 1 Corinthians 13. This word is "charity"—a form of a specific self-denying love but with distinct differences from the general meaning of deep emotional, or affectionate love.

The King James Bible translators allowed, due to context, a definitive translation term for agape in 1 Corinthians 13. "Love" is a subjective term of deep emotion and as such carries a wide range of nuances and meanings. A father's love for a son is not the same quality as his 'love' of a sport. The love that exists between a married couple is not the same as their joint love for longstanding family ownership of property. Context between experiences determines how love differs or is alike.

The context of 1 Corinthians 13 demands that the "agape" found and described there must demand a different word than the normal "love." For example, the translated term agape in the 1 Corinthians context demands: Precedence and importance of it over speech ability (13:1) prophecy, faith, (13:2) generosity and personal physical suffering (13:3), and demands longsuffering.

Charity also demands kindness, an absence of envy, self-denial, (13:4) the presence of good behavior, assumption of no iniquity in others, bears-believes-hopes and endures all things (13:5-7) never fails (13:8) and is greater than faith and hope.

The translators chose the word "charity"; the context demands it is not the secular charity of giving to benevolent causes, it is higher than that.

1 Corinthians 13:3 And though I bestow all my goods to feed the poor, and though I give my body to be burned, and have not charity, it profiteth me nothing.

It is even greater than personal faith! Another passage where agape is translated charity:

Colossians 3:14 And above all these things put on charity, which is the bond of perfectness.

Charity is a unique form of love, the bond of perfection that every believer should strive to exercise with all other believers.

When we consider that the very essence of God is agape (love), and that instead of the love of God "enduring all things"- the love of God demands payment for sin—it is evident that the agape of 1 Corinthians 13 is different from Deity's agape toward sinners and demands a more definitive form of agape: charity.

IS THE LORD'S COMING NEAR OR NIGH?

A translation rule employed by the King James Bible: Contextual interpretation that provides definitive meaning to a term is superior to a translation based on a general vocabulary meaning.

General translation methods only give a primary or basic meaning of a source word: Greek (in this case: ἐγγύς) into the target language (English). All modern versions follow the general method. However, proper translation of a word also requires an *interpretational translation* of the word's contextual use. Consideration of how it is used in the near context provides understanding. In other words, Matthew 24 translated by the NIV reads:

"As Jesus was sitting on the Mount of Olives, the disciples came to him privately. "Tell us," they said, "when will this happen, and what will be the sign of your coming and of the end of the age?" (Matthew 24:3 New International Version)

"Now learn this lesson from the fig tree: As soon as its twigs get tender and its leaves come out, you know that summer is near. 33 Even so, when you see all these things, you know that it is near, right at the door." (Matthew 24:32-33 New International Version)

The NASV, ESV, CSB, RSV, and the NKJV all read the same as the NIV. All of these translations are "one legged": they generally translate but omit the contextual interpretation of the terms. Thus, the full understanding of "near" and "nigh" by their readers is blurred and never understood.

On the other hand, the King James Bible stands on both legs: translation governed by contextual interpretation. The context of this parable of the fig tree is found in Jesus' reply to the questions, "when" and "what":

"And as he sat upon the mount of Olives, the disciples came

unto him privately, saying, Tell us, when shall these things be? and what *shall be* the sign of thy coming, and of the end of the world?" (Matthew 24:3 KJB)

"Now learn a parable of the fig tree; When his branch is yet tender, and putteth forth leaves, ye know that summer *is* nigh: 33 So likewise ye, when ye shall see all these things, know that it is near, *even* at the doors." (Matthew 24:32-33 KJB)

The disciples' questions are threefold:

1. When shall these things be? The Lord answers question one in Matthew 24:4-32.

2. What shall be the sign of thy coming? Questions 2 and 3 are answered in verses 32-33.

3. What shall be the sign of the end of the world? ("world" is a Bible word that may mean people, age, economy, or a period of time—which definitive meaning depends upon near usage context.)

The sign of His coming is NIGH *(close but not immediately ready to appear)* at first with the many occurring signs of a summer season. The sign of the end of the world is NEAR—when the detailed signs are finished ("when ye see ALL these things…": false christs, prophets, wars, etc., of Matthew 24:3-23) His coming is at the door—the world's age ends immediately after his coming.

"Nigh" is the KJB English meaning *"close but not adjacent to or in a near proximity"*. When the fig tree branch is yet tender (not fully matured) and the leaves (putteth: the KJB -eth indicates a continual present action) are beginning to sprout, summer will be coming soon—but when you see "ALL these things" i.e., all events combined as described throughout the chapter, then "IT" (the time of His Second Coming) is standing at Heaven's door, about to enter.

As noted above, only using "the Greek" without consideration of the context can produce a poor translation. The various definitions found in Strong's Concordance (below) demonstrate the definitive weakness.

"ἐγγὺς (Greek) Strong's: From a primary verb ἄγχω agchō (to *squeeze* or *throttle*; akin to the base of G43); *near* (literally or figuratively, of place or time): - from, at hand, near, nigh (at hand, unto), ready."

Thus, a general (lacking inerrancy) of an English translation of Matthew 24:32-33 *might possibly* be called THE NEWEST NEW INTERGALACTIC VERSION and could read:

"Now learn a parable of the fig tree; When his branch is yet tender, and putteth forth leaves, ye know that summer *is* <u>READY</u> (from Strong's concordance): 33 So likewise ye, when ye shall see all these things, know that it is <u>AT HAND</u>, *even* at the doors." (Matthew 24:32-33 NNGV)

The same is true in the Old Testament.

"And Moses alone shall come near the LORD: but they shall not come nigh; neither shall the people go up with him." (Exodus 24:2 KJB)

"nâgash (Hebrew) Strong's: A primitive root; to *be* or *come* (causatively *bring*) *near* (for any purpose); euphemistically to *lie with* a woman; as an enemy, to *attack*; religiously to *worship*; causatively to *present*; figuratively to *adduce* an argument; by reversal, to *stand back:* - (make to) approach (nigh), bring (forth, hither, near), (cause to) come (higher, near, nigh), give place, go hard (up), (be, draw, go) near (nigh), offer, overtake, present, put, stand."

From the Hebrew word "*nagash*"(*as defined by Strong*) it is easy to see how a modern translation may be generally 'correct' (*<u>as far as a translation goes, but without proper contextual interpretation, meaning, or sense)</u>* and read in Exodus 24:2:

"**And Moses alone shall** *approach* **the LORD: but they shall not** *approach* **; neither shall the people** *stand back* **with him.**"

 <u>*Interpretation by any vocabulary meaning alone*</u> results in a poor or even inaccurate translation. The CSB joins the NIV as an illustration of the poor translation method:

"**but Moses alone is to approach the LORD; the others must not come near. And the people may not come up with him.**"
(Exodus24:2 New International Version)
"**Moses alone is to approach the LORD, but the others are not to approach, and the people are not to go up with him.**"
(Exodus 24:2 Christian Standard Bible)
 The people do not know whether they are "coming" or "going" in the NIV and CSB !!

 The English of the King James Bible is unique and precise in that it is a biblically definitive English; this is accomplished by contextual, interpretive translation.

BUILT and BUILDED in the KJB or BUILT in the NIV and CSB?

"For every house is built by someone, but God is the builder of everything." (Hebrews 3:4 New International Version) "Now every house is built by someone, but the one who built everything is God." (Hebrews 3:4 Christian Standard Bible)

The following text from a 1608 book has been edited to reflect modern print fonts instead of 17th Century letter fonts:

"…a man could not easily climb or pass over it. Also there were certain which made such steep steps without any ditch which they named walls, and they of old time also named that a BUILDED enclosure, which was made of dry stones or slate laid upon one another, and that in divers forms: for either the same was made with clay and stones, workmanly and finely BUILT (in those places especially) by which quarries of stone were near unto…" (Thomas Hill, *The Arte of Gardening*. Printed by Edward Allde, London. 1608. p. 24.)

This 1608 book recognizes the difference in the definitive meanings of built and builded (past participles). Unfortunately, since 1901 English Bible versions have lost the difference by treating "builded" as archaic.

An incomplete, or ongoing, unfinished work, with multiple elements is **BUILDED**. When reference is made to a whole, complete, finished, and final structure, **BUILT** is the proper participle. This illustrates a superior quality of 1600-1900 English over contemporary English — it is more definitive.

Another example is found in the following poem:

"There stands Abydos ! — here is Sestos' steep,
Hard by the gusty margin of the sea,
Where sprinkling waves continually do leap ;
And that is where those famous lovers be,

A builded gloom shot up into the grey,
    As if the first tall watch-tow'r of the day."

(Walter Jerrold, *The Complete Poetical Works of Thomas Hood*
1906. Oxford University Press, Amen Corner, E.C. III 170.)

The King James Bible (KJB) contains this definitive difference between the meanings of builded and built in many places both in the OT and NT. Builded: A participle that refers to the work of man, an incomplete, ongoing, unfinished with multiple elements. Built: A participle that refers to the whole, complete, finished, and final structure.

"Then king Asa made a proclamation throughout all Judah; none was exempted: and they took away the stones of Ramah, and the timber thereof, wherewith Baasha had builded; and king Asa built with them Geba of Benjamin, and Mizpah." (1 Kings 15:22 KJB)

"I made me great works; I builded me houses; I planted me vineyards:"
(Ecclesiastes 2:4 KJB)

"For every house is builded by some *man;* but he that built all things *is* God." (Hebrews 3:4 KJB)

The American Standard Version of 1901 agreed with the King James Bible: a temporal house builded by man's labor depends on God's created elements and does not last like those things built by God.

"For every house is builded by some one; but he that built all things is God."
(Hebrews 3:4 ASV 1901)

Unfortunately, the Christian Standard Bible in Hebrews 3:4 is "up to snuff" with modern English participle usage but claims that man's work is the same as God's work:

"Now every house is built by someone, but the one who built everything is God." (Hebrews 3:4 Christian Standard Bible)

CORRECT OR COMMUNICATIVE SPEECH?

There is a great difference between being *correct* in your grammar, speech, technical terms and in your *communication* of all its facts to your hearers. Correctness or Communication? Which is best?

Most *hearers* of a speech about a NASA flight plans do not care for correctness of technical details or even the speaker's proper grammar, but the space flight's participants definitely would. Those who are not conversant with specific "terms of the trade" have no interest in knowing why the azimuth is expressed as the angular distance from the north or south point of the horizon to the point at which a vertical circle passes through the object intersecting the horizon.

Of course, all of this is 'perfectly clear' by further clarification from Wikipedia: "Used in celestial navigation, an *azimuth* is the direction of a celestial body from the observer. In astronomy, an *azimuth* is <u>sometimes</u> referred to as a <u>bearing</u>. In modern <u>astronomy</u> azimuth is <u>nearly always</u> measured from the north. (The article on <u>coordinate systems</u>, for example, uses a convention measuring from the south.) In former times, it was common to refer to azimuth from the south, as it was then zero at the same time that the <u>hour angle</u> of a <u>star</u> was zero. This <u>assumes</u>, however, that the star <u>(upper) culminates</u> in the south, <u>which is only true</u> if the star's <u>declination</u> is less than (i.e. further south than) the observer's <u>latitude</u>."

Communicative speech is totally different. "We are going on a ship to the 20th degree longitude on the equator's latitude. From there we will use a compass, directed towards the true north of the earth and through the planet Mars position. Using an algebraic formula, that will give us the approximate direction from the equator to Mars." *If that is not clear to the audience, there is no possibility of a clearer explanation.*

The preference is correct information that communicates truth. A few eyebrows will surely be raised and perhaps several frowns will cross critical visages over the following statement: "The King James Bible, unlike other English translations of scripture, offers a pure blend of translation accuracy of its words along with a communication of the meaning of those inspired words to the dedicated reader."

The former reference to "compass" is a prime example of the communicative accuracy of the King James Bible (KJB). "Compass" — the noun or verb form — appears 127 times in the KJB. The term is defined by the contexts of Joshua 6 and 2 Chronicles 4.

"And ye shall compass the city, all *ye* men of war, *and* go round about the city once. Thus shalt thou do six days. 4 And seven priests shall bear before the ark seven trumpets of rams' horns: and the seventh day ye shall compass the city seven times, and the priests shall blow with the trumpets." (Joshua 6:3-4 KJB)

"Moreover he made an altar of brass, twenty cubits the length thereof, and twenty cubits the breadth thereof, and ten cubits the height thereof. 2 Also he made a molten sea of ten cubits from brim to brim, round in compass, and five cubits the height thereof; and a line of thirty cubits did compass it round about. 3 And under it *was* the similitude of oxen, which did compass it round about: ten in a cubit, compassing the sea round about. Two rows of oxen *were* cast, when it was cast. 4 It stood upon twelve oxen, three looking toward the north, and three looking toward the west, and three looking toward the south, and three looking toward the east: and the sea *was set* above upon them, and all their hinder parts *were* inward." (2 Chronicles 4:1-4 KJB)

The context of both is clear: to "compass" is not a reference to getting an object or thing. The word is a verb of an action or adverb describing the action. In Joshua "compass the city" is described as "go round about the city". In 2 Chronicles the "sea" (contained water) has a circumference of "ten cubits from brim to brim, round in compass".

The plus 20 volumed Oxford English Dictionary that records centuries of English usage gives meanings for the noun, verb, and adverb forms of the term, compassed, compass, compassion. The verb and adverb forms are defined:

1. To come round, close round, as a multitude; to form a circle about, surround, with friendly or hostile intent; to hem in; sometimes spec. 'to beleaguer, besiege, block' (Johnson).
2. To go or come round, put round, encompass.

Number 1 usage: **"And when the servant of the man of God was risen early, and gone forth, behold, an host compassed the city both with horses and chariots. And his servant said unto him, Alas, my master! how shall we do?" (2 Kings 6:15 KJB)**

Number 2 usage: **"Then we turned, and took our journey into the wilderness by the way of the Red sea, as the LORD spake unto me: and we compassed mount Seir many days." (Deuteronomy 2:1 KJB)** *(Israel did not surround the mountain, they traveled around it.)*

The usage of "fetch a compass" as an adverbial phrase in Acts 26:13, means to take an <u>extended</u> ("fetch", as opposed to the more general verb "get" or "take") circuitous trip.

"And from thence we fetched a compass, and came to Rhegium: and after one day the south wind blew, and we came the next day to Puteoli:" (Acts 28:13 KJB)

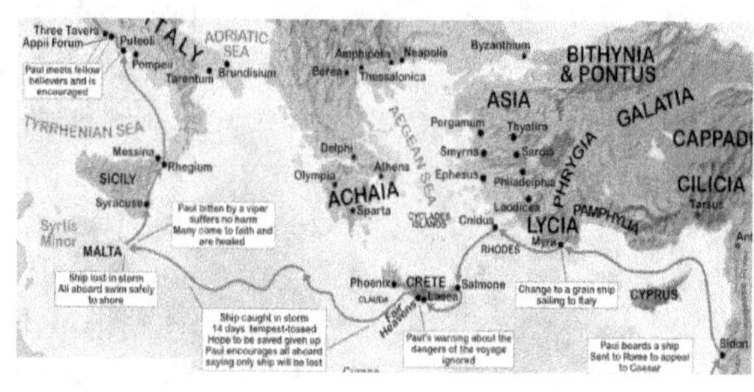

You could buy a map of the First Century Mediterranean Sea and locate Puteoli but the most economical way is to simply let the KJB define what "fetch a compass" means.

Or, you could buy a NIV and get the short and less informative account of the irregular, circuitous coastline trip from Syracuse to Puteoli:

"From there we set sail and arrived at Rhegium. The next day the south wind came up, and on the following day we reached Puteoli." (Acts 28:13 New International Version).

(The Chinese are credited with the first <u>instrument</u> to note the earth's WNES layout, a "compass", which was used in feng shui geomancy practice around 200AD rather than use in travel orientation or direction. A Chinese compass consisted of a magnetic lodestone in shape of a spoon upon a flat surface. The heavier scooped spoon portion pointed to the magnetic North earth pole while the lessor weighted spoon handle pointed South. Failing to need or see the importance of the North pole coupled with the Chinese custom of reading from clockwise and bottom up, the South pole direction of the handle was reckoned in Chinese culture more important than the North pointing spoon. The geomancy reading claimed to use energy forces that harmonized individuals with their surrounding environment. In classical feng shui philosophy, a house should face the West, that direction supposedly being favorable to the future and childbearing.)

THE SINGULAR PRONOUN (T) OR PLURAL PRONOUN (Y): DOES IT REALLY MATTER?

THEE AND YOU PRONOUNS

The King James Bible (KJB) has within its text helpful Greek grammar lessons. Most common are the English pronouns that begin with a "T" and the pronouns that begin with "Y". Greek pronouns are either singular in number (one person or collective group: T) or plural in number (two or more: Y).

When the KJB has "thee", "thy", "thine", etc., the Greek pronoun is of singular number; when we read "you", "your", etc., the Greek pronoun is a plural number. This feature is valuable in understanding or interpreting certain passages. An example is in the letter from Paul to Philemon; the pronouns are commented on and noted by italics.

"Paul, a prisoner of Jesus Christ, and Timothy our brother, unto Philemon (the letter is addressed specifically to Philemon) our dearly beloved, and fellowlabourer, 2 And to our beloved Apphia, and Archippus our fellowsoldier, and to the church in thy house *(Philemon is to convey greetings to several others)* **3 Grace to you, (To all; Apphia, Archippus and the church group) and peace, from God our Father and the Lord Jesus Christ. 4 I thank my God, making mention of thee** *(specifically of Philemon)* **always in my prayers, 5 Hearing of thy** *(Philemon's)* **love and faith, which thou** *(Philemon's)* **hast toward the Lord Jesus, and toward all saints; 6 That the communication of thy** *(Philemon's righteous works)* **faith may become effectual by the acknowledging of every good thing which is in you (all of them) in Christ Jesus. 7 For we have great joy and consolation in thy** *(Paul now begins to direct his reason for writing to Philemon)* **love, because the bowels of the saints are refreshed by thee,** *(Philemon)* **brother.**

8 Wherefore, though I might be much bold in Christ to enjoin thee *(Paul now specifies the issue to Philemon)* that which is convenient,
9 Yet for love's sake I rather beseech thee, *(the reason for the letter and the issue between Philemon, Onesimus, and Paul)* being such an one as Paul the aged, and now also a prisoner of Jesus Christ.
10 I beseech thee for my son Onesimus, whom I have begotten in my bonds:
11 Which in time past was to thee *(Onesimus caused some problem to Philemon)* unprofitable, but now profitable to thee *(Something has made Onesimus no longer a problem)* and to me:
12 Whom I have sent again: thou therefore receive him, that is, mine own bowels:
13 Whom I would have retained with me, that in thy stead he might have ministered unto me in the bonds of the gospel:
14 But without thy mind would I do nothing; that thy benefit should not be as it were of necessity, but willingly.
15 For perhaps he therefore departed for a season, that thou shouldest receive him for ever;
16 Not now as a servant, but above a servant, a brother beloved, specially to me, but how much more unto thee, both in the flesh, and in the Lord?
17 If thou count me therefore a partner, receive him as myself.
18 If he hath wronged thee, or oweth thee ought, put that on mine account;
19 I Paul have written it with mine own hand, I will repay it: albeit I do not say to thee how thou owest unto me even thine own self besides.
20 Yea, brother, let me have joy of thee in the Lord: refresh my bowels in the Lord." (Philemon 1-20 KJB)

This small book of Philemon closes the letters of Paul with a grand illustration of one of Paul's major themes: justification of a sinner by the faith of Another, Jesus Christ.

Onesimus was "unprofitable" in the past to Philemon

and departed for that reason. But God providentially brought Paul and Onesimus together. Onesimus became a "brother", evidently by the gospel witness of Paul. Now Paul reminds and beseeches Philemon to receive Onesimus and if he owes Philemon anything, Paul entreats Onesimus to put it on Paul's account.

Another example of the need for a distinction between plural and singular pronouns is found in Luke 22:31-32:

31 "And the Lord said, Simon, Simon, behold, Satan hath desired to have you, *(Satan already had one of the disciples, Judas. Satan desired to have all of the disciples)* **that he may sift** *you* **as wheat:**

32 But I have prayed for thee, *(Simon, as leader of the disciples, when his faith did not fail, he could strengthen his brethren)* **that thy faith fail not: and when thou art converted, strengthen thy brethren."** *(It does not require many to strengthen many — but one converted man can strengthen many.)*

IS THERE CLARITY IN THE NEW INTERNATIONAL VERSION OR THE CHRISTIAN STANDARD BIBLE ?

"Simon, Simon, Satan has asked to sift all of you as wheat. But I have prayed for you, Simon, that your faith may not fail. And when you have turned back, strengthen your brothers." (Luke 22:31-32 New International Version)
According to the NIV, Satan asked to sift ALL OF YOU (i.e., all 12 of the Apostles).

"Simon, Simon, look out. Satan has asked to sift you like wheat. 32 But I have prayed for you that your faith may not fail. And you, when you have turned back, strengthen your brothers." (Luke 22:31-32 Christian Standard Bible)
According to the CSB, it is not clear whether Satan asked to sift ALL OF YOU (i.e., all 12 of the Apostles) or only Simon.

Simon is the spokesman for the twelve and the Lord addressed him as the spokesman –not as a separate individual Apostle. Who has the Lord prayed for? All the Apostles or only Simon? Perhaps Simon.

According to the NIV's specificity by name : "**But I have prayed for you, <u>Simon</u>, that your faith may not fail**" there is no doubt for whom the Lord prayed. But the CSB omits the specificity of the Lord's prayer, and only says: "**But I have prayed for you…**"

The KJB translation is clear:

31 "And the Lord said, Simon, Simon, behold, Satan hath desired to have you, *(Satan already had one of the disciples, Judas. Satan desired to have all)* **that he may sift** *you* **as wheat: 32 But I have prayed for thee,** *(Simon, as leader of the disciples, when his faith did not fail, he did strengthen his brethren)* **that thy faith fail not: and when thou art converted, strengthen thy brethren."** *(It does not require many to strengthen many — but one converted man can strengthen many.)*

GENDER POLITICS

"The updated NIV you now have in your hands builds on both the original NIV and the TNIV and represents the latest effort of the committee to articulate God's unchanging Word in the way the original authors might have said it had they been speaking in English to the global English-speaking audience today." (NIV 2011 preface)

This is one of several erroneous assumptions by the CBT (Committee on Bible Translation) of the NIV and has led the work into a morass of doctrinal confusion. One glaring example is the CBT's obsession with the feminist/politically correct terms. One assumption is that *"the global English-speaking audience today"* is all onboard with the gender sensitive attitude of 2022 USA liberalism. One surprise may be the different Hispanic role attitude of "mommas and poppas" of our southern border neighbors, or the different Asian view expressed by over 2/3s of the world's peoples who speak and read English as a second language.

The 12 Apostles are all male *so far* but watch out--the next NIV might have Barbie replacing Thomas or Betsy instead of Matthew. Anyhow, here is what has happened:

"3 So watch yourselves. If your brother or sister [FN] sins against you, rebuke them; and if they repent, forgive them." (Luke 17:3 New International Version)

NIV Footnote to Luke 17:3: "Luke 17:3 The Greek word for brother or sister (adelphos) refers here to a fellow disciple, whether man or woman."

WOW!! What a misleading footnote! How non-informative!! The footnote simply corrupts what the text said: "brother or sister". "Adelphos" is NOT the Greek word for a brother or a sister as the NIV's parenthetical insert claims. Every first year Greek student knows that the alpha prefix (ἀ-) on the Greek substantive (womb -δελφός) means a human <u>without a womb</u> , the distinction being determined by Bible context .

I say "corrupt text" because the NIV translators corrupted the text by their footnote definition of the Greek "adelphos" and that the KJB translation of "brother" can <u>only</u> mean a male. Here is the Bible text:

"3 Take heed to yourselves: If thy brother trespass against thee, rebuke him; and if he repent, forgive him." (Luke 17:3 KJB)

The NIV blunder is called "gender inclusive" language. In other words, we must take out the long-understood (by context) terms like mother, sister, brother, man, woman, etc. and replace them with gender neutral words. God forbid that the man be the head of the woman! Even though the Bible declares it, the "political view changes" in English demands that we change the Bible. The Greek words in the New Testament are man, woman, brother, sister, etc., but we are supposed to accept the blundering NIV's lame explanation that since views have changed-- even God has changed His mind on the gender issue.

Therefore, it means nothing that Adam was first created and is head of the human race (composed of males and females) and woman in a marriage relationship, or that Christ chose Twelve male apostles. We are assured by the NIV that had the 12 been chosen today, there would have been equal female/male representation. This conbobulational theology found in the NIV *in many instances* is as far from biblical revelation as a jackass' barnyard braying is from a Luciano Pavarotti performance at Concert Hall.

Have you ever wondered why:
Adam was made before Eve? God made Adam of the dust of the ground but made Eve from a rib of Adam?
Noah was chosen to lead in building the ark? Why not Mrs. Noah?
The Patriarchs of Israel were Abraham, Isaac, and Jacob? Why not the matriarchs: Sarah, Rebekah or Rachel?

Moses was chosen to lead Israel and given the 10 Commandments? Even though he was not sinless?
All tribes of Israel called by male names and led by males?
Why Joshua was chosen—instead of "Josephine" as Moses successor?
Why all Major Prophets are male as well as all Minor Prophets? Why did God not choose Miriam, Deborah, Huldah, etc.—were they not prophetesses?
God called John the Baptist? Did he discriminate by not calling "Johnine"?
12 Apostles are all males?
God called Paul instead of "Paulette"?

Is God a discriminator of people? Does God discriminate between good and bad? Righteous and unholy? Do you not "judge" or make discriminations between this or that every day? When the traffic light is red, do you judge between stopping or running it?

Have you ever surmised there might be a doctrinal reason for all this 'maleness' in scripture? Is it not possible that God emphasizes man and woman in various Bible passages due to different responsibility and function issues between a male and female? Isn't it also not possible for God to also use "man" to represent the ALL of both sexes of all mankind?

Does the word "wo-man" mean a human being with a womb or a help to match or meet the reproductive process? Even a redneck country boy knows that mules do not reproduce and that a bull and a cow are more profitable than only two cows. To plainly speak, If God had made "Adam" and "Steve" instead of Adam and Eve, you would not be around to argue!

Without agreeing with all Southern Baptist Convention (SBC) doctrines, we do agree with a branch that sees the difficulty in criticism of biblical genders.

The Council on Biblical Manhood and Womanhood (CBMW) is the flagship organization for SBC complementarianism. *Complementarians believe God created man male and female, equal in dignity and worth, different in role in the family and the church.*

CBMW argues that for centuries, Bible readers have had no problem applying to a wider audience, specific biblical passages that focus only on one gender. The danger in the 2011 translation philosophy, CBMW said in its evaluation, is in the translators changing "the meaning and the application of the text in ways that they may not intend or even realize."

"Our main concern is that in hundreds of places, meaning in the Bible is eroded because of the translators' decisions to remove words like he, him, his, father, brother, son, and man," Randy Stinson, CBMW president, told Baptist Press in an email interview. He also serves as dean of the school of church ministries at Southern Baptist Theological Seminary. "God's Word is the product of his infinite wisdom and all the details of meaning are there for a purpose. ... Evangelicals have long believed that all Scripture is breathed out by God. This extends to every word of Scripture, not just basic thoughts."

The "original authors" of the Bible did not accommodate their readers' ignorance, whims, or socio/political agendas—neither did the translators in 1611. The NIV has confused scriptural accuracy with social palatability. Translation is not making the message palatable; it is passing the original message on—unadulterated.

Translation is not sweetening the message; translation is serving it up as it came out of the kitchen. To add A-1 sauce to a premium steak is an insult to the chef but that is what the NIV has done to God's revelation and the Revelator!

It is as if they took a 1937 D-27 $8,000.00 Martin guitar and put on 1990 Sears Roebuck tuning keys, a plastic nut and bridge in place of ivory, dug the mother of pearl inlays out, put play dough in and put on fifty year old ukulele strings found in a Waikiki Beach garbage can-- and called the garbage a better masterpiece.

Here is another linguistic marvel: levels of translation are not the same into every target language. And this brings up the fact that hundreds of languages (includes different dialects 2019) do not have a verse translated into their tongue. If Biblica (parent company of NIV) is really serious about the need "to articulate God's unchanging Word" at least some of this energy and money spent on duplicity of English translation should be directed towards those who have not ever heard even one of God's words! Of course, tribal groups don't have much dinero or USD to pay for a "Kasava Bread NIV (Recipes for Kasava and Burning Relatives)" or "The War Group NIV" and "Young Jungle Mother's NIV."

Translation is not making all Bible passages so easy to read that ALL its words and sentence meanings are understood BY ALL at first glance. The "dumbed-down" Bible translations are miserable failures. Please don't misunderstand me here. A translation should be clear and accurate but to attempt to make it so simple that everyone within one reading understands everything — is not scriptural--nor is it possible.

The word of God has milk for the beginner but within its pages there is also bread and meat for the serious student. God intends for some passages to require study, comparison, and also leave deliberate confusion for the careless and sceptic reader.

SERVANT or SLAVE

"Paul, a servant of Jesus Christ, called to be an apostle, separated unto the gospel of God," (Romans 1:1 KJB)
"Paul, a slave of Christ Jesus and called to be an apostle, set apart for God's good news," (Romans 1:1 NWT: Jehovah's Witness New Testament)

Greek allows δουλος to be translated either as "slave" or "servant" depending upon the usage context. There is quite a bit of difference in meaning between the two. Slavery is a forced condition that does not allow a personal choice of work, it is dictated by another; a servant has personal liberty and is allowed a freedom of choice to serve or not to serve.

Paul is a willing *servant* of Jesus Christ and delights in that position rather than any other title. It is not proper to use "slave" with reference to a saved person, because a "slave" is a person who has a forced, indentured relationship to a master, totally against his will. There is nothing in Bible doctrine that implies the Christian life or ministry is slavery. To claim an office of apostle, pastor, or deacon is slavery may imply unwilling service.

The term "slavery" is used by some emotional Bible commentators so as to sound more "spiritual" or to imply a more dedicated position than a servant *(So it seems to me)*. A Christian is not without a will, very possibly not always faithful, and can serve or resist, doubt or believe, waste his life, or redeem the time; all point to the poor translation of δουλος when describing a saved person.

We were not captured or bought as a piece of property into a forced indenture. We were bought with a price far above any type of worldly property transaction and loved with divine, unconditional love.

Our relationship to God is a SON--*NOT AS A SLAVE.* We are "born of God"; we are in the household of God, not as an unwilling slave but a willing Son, members in His body.

The reason for translating the Greek word "doulos" as "servant" is because the position is a willing one. A son may choose to be a servant by gratitude, thankfulness, but he can not choose to be a slave because unlike servant, a slave is void of familial relationship.

"Slave" has in its etymological Celtic language history the idea of "being driven", that is, against the will. It is a disgusting term one would use of himself to describe a unwilling, but forced situation. This practice of translating "doulos" as slave comes not from the context of God's word, or even Greek/English usage.

In my opinion only, the reason a Bible translation would translate Paul as a "slave of Christ Jesus" (NWT) in Romans 1 is a translation or teaching by a religious group such as the Jehovah's Witnesses that views the Christian life as requiring a forced servitude for salvation. Otherwise, without the group's prescribed works for salvation, the members would lose, or fail to gain eternal salvation.

FAITH AND BELIEF

Belief: The English word, belief, as a verb (believe) is a mental action of trust, assurance, and carries the idea to rely upon, to rest upon, to accept as true. Belief does not require a physical work or involvement to exist, it is simply an acceptance of truth.

Faith: The English word, faith, includes belief, but faith also requires a physical work or material action in order to exist. Faith without the accompanying element of a physical work does not exist.

The 22 volume Oxford English Dictionary is the authoritative dictionary for usage of English terms from 1200AD to the present. In its volumes "faith" is defined to *contain* the mental assent to trust, assurance, and belief, but it also requires a physical, material work of duty or fulfillment.

Therefore, when we read the English word "belief" we should never confuse it with the word "faith" and vice versa. This definitive word difference is found in the word of God, the King James Bible. To recognize the difference between the two words produces a more complete and accurate understanding of bible doctrine throughout the various periods of time.

Just as all men of all periods of time throughout the bible are saved by grace, so the same men are only saved by faith. The questions that must be answered by scripture are: "What 'faith work'? "Whose 'faith'? It is easy to understand that unless the God's grace allows, permits, and accepts sinful men, no one could be saved. Saved by faith is not so easy to understand because there are two major faiths in the bible, and there are at least four qualities of one of them.

TWO FAITHS IN THE KING JAMES BIBLE

The faith of a man

The Faith of God*

(Faith is the quality of the work of the Second Person of the Godhead, the Lord Jesus Christ, His sinless life and vicarious death.)

There are four/five kinds of man's faith *(Belief accompanied by works acceptable to God)*:
Weak faith**

Little faith***

Great faith****

Full faith*****

#Dead faith# *(Belief composed of works not accepted by God)*

*Galatians 2:16 Knowing that a man is not justified by the works of the law, but by the <u>faith of Jesus Christ</u>, even <u>we have believed in Jesus Christ</u>, that we might be justified by <u>the faith of Christ</u>, and not by the works of the law: for by the works of the law shall no flesh be justified.

**Romans 14:1 Him that is <u>weak in the faith</u> receive ye, *but* not to doubtful disputations.

***Matthew 6:30 Wherefore, if God so clothe the grass of the field, which to day is, and to morrow is cast into the oven, *shall he* not much more *clothe* you, O ye of <u>little faith</u>?

****Matthew 8:10 When Jesus heard *it*, he marvelled, and said to them that followed, Verily I say unto you, I have not found so <u>great faith</u>, no, not in Israel.

*****Acts 6:8 And Stephen, <u>full of faith</u> and power, did great wonders and miracles among the people.

#James 2:17 Even so faith, if it hath not works, is <u>dead</u>, being alone.

James 2:18 Yea, a man may say, Thou hast faith, and I have works: shew me thy faith without thy works, and <u>I will shew thee my faith by my works</u>.

THE GOSPEL OF GRACE DEMANDS BELIEF WITH NO REQUIREMENT OF A WORK BY MAN

The Bible was never planned by God to read like a kindergarten book. While the essential doctrines are simply stated, other teaching requires dedicated study for understanding. Those who fail to believe the simple doctrines, stumble into error, and find confusion with the more complicated doctrines.

Also, the Bible was given to be carefully read — all of it! Reading from Genesis to Revelation reveals a divine structure, plan, and purpose for all of its words and 66 books. The Bible was never meant to be cut up into an isolated verse here or there and treated as some magical talisman to bring good luck.

Although the Bible warns against changing, adding to, or subtracting any of its words, it never claims that every person of every period of time or age, is to obey every command or instruction. In other words, there is a divine plan constructed by the Author so that the reader can understand that certain instructions are given to some men, while the same are not given to all men. This is emphasized by the required study of right division of the text. In other words, the Bible is divided into different doctrines or even different ages of the creation.

Which in other ages was not made known unto the sons of men, as it is now revealed unto his holy apostles and prophets by the Spirit; (Ephesians 3:5 KJB)

"Other ages" of men that did not know, contrasted with "now revealed" demands past various ages with different doctrines or instructions. One age differs from the following in some doctrine and instructions.

Study to shew thyself approved unto God, a workman that needeth not to be ashamed, rightly dividing the word of truth. (2 Timothy 2:15 KJB)

Notice two words: Study and workman. This command to study and work at it, is placed after Bible ages have passed. The direction to "rightly divide" does not add or subtract any doctrine or instruction to past ages but it _separates_ the present age from the past ages without any criticism of the past. This allows different instructions or doctrines between the past ages and present one — but permits integrity to all the ages. Simply put: division is a math operation that does not add or subtract from 12 when divided by 2. Proper division allows more understanding of 12: we understand by dividing 12 by 2 equals 6, therefore, there are two sixes in twelve! The number 12 is not changed, but more understanding of its composition is gained.

This command to rightly divide comes at a conspicuous place: after other ages. This is a divine indication that the present age is in some way drastically different than past ages. Modern translations muddy the orthographic waters when they change "dividing" to "handling." Dividing is more definitive than handling; handling is a generality but dividing is a specific verb of action.

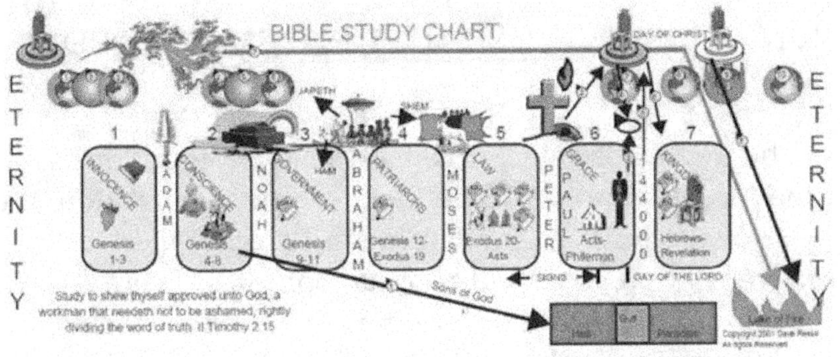

The chart above shows the various ages of time (a total of 7). Every age is similar in some respects of doctrine but differs from the others in certain doctrines and instructions. For example in age number 1 (Innocence), the murderer is protected but in age number 2 throughout others the murderer is to be executed. Another example is with celebration of one day of the week over another day: No "rest" or sabbath day is directed for man from Age 1 (Innocence) until the 5th Age (Law). Then, in the 6th Age (Grace) any distinction or celebration of one day over others of a week is forbidden!

Let no man therefore judge you in meat, or in drink, or in respect of an holyday, or of the new moon, or of the sabbath *days:*

Which are a shadow of things to come; but the body *is* of Christ. (Colossians 2:16-17 KJB)

The 6th Age does not forbid celebration of a certain day, neither does it not command it either! Instead, the word of God gives a man living under grace the permission to live in a "shadow" of doctrine (instead of the light) if he wills to do so. At the same time, the KJB says special day observance will return in a future age. Read Hebrews through Revelation in the KJB to see the return of holy days.

THE KING JAMES BIBLE METHODOLOGY OF WORD DEFINITIONS

The translators were given a rule to avoid footnotes and time has proven that guideline to be more of wisdom than simply a royal whim of King James who did not like the Geneva translation, mainly due to its footnotes. There appears to be several reasons why the King did not like the Geneva version, its copious footnotes being only one.

Footnotes by necessity are the views of men, and views of men are affected by their individual beliefs. This limits the inspired word of God to a denominational or narrow meaning of certain theological doctrines. The Calvinistic influence upon the Genevan translators overwhelmed certain bible doctrines and the footnotes dictated Calvinism's system to be the only view. Total depravity of man was emphasized so that man had no will of his own; unconditional election; limited atonement of Christ, all of these plus other interpretations were reflected in footnotes.

The AV1611 translation followed a different path. The KJB left the usage of a word or phrase to be defined in the context of its use in scripture rather than the definition of a word in the mind of a man or group of men.

By omitting footnotes, the KJB also allowed the number of times a word is used in scripture to be self-defining. By using a Bible concordance, the reader can find the number of instances the same word is used in a variety of scripture contexts. By looking up all the occurrences of the word, the usage will reveal the definition.

Parallelism is another feature of allowing scripture to define itself. The same phrase or sentence is repeated in other words. For example:

She crieth at the <u>gates</u>, at the <u>entry</u> of the city, at the <u>coming in at the doors</u>. (Proverbs 8:3 KJB)

Gate is defined as "the entry", the place of "the coming in."

The parallelism may define by contrast:

Whoso <u>despiseth the word</u> shall be destroyed: but he that <u>feareth the commandment</u> shall be rewarded. (Proverbs 13:13 KJB)

By the above means, the KJB bears its own dictionary.

WHAT PROMPTS THE MODERN TRANSLATORS TO BE KJB CRITICS?

Besides money, I believe the urge to correct the King James Bible words with some modern translation has an underlying, perhaps even unknowing motive: evolution. The basic definition of biological evolutionary doctrine is that different kinds of living organisms have developed and diversified from earlier forms during the history of the earth. This development is assumed to be a better one in the new than the former or old development. The evolutionary guesswork has affected all fields of science. It reasons, "Has not man developed into an upright intellect from a hunched back, slobbering, knuckle-dragging ape?" "Isn't the Bible a collection of archaic folk tales repeated around a fire?" "Is our science not more accurate today than 5 centuries ago?" "Has not language changed in the past century?"

The answer to all this is that it is true that knowledge or man's so-called science has increased. It is not true that man himself has increased in quality over the ages. Over 6,000 years of history has not removed murder, rape, incest, robbery, adultery, hatred, envy, etc., etc., from mankind daily lives.

It is clear that 'evolution' (even if true) cannot always mean an increase for the better.

History proves "devolution" in many areas. "Knowing more or able to understand more" does not mean a better quality of life.

Some of the most miserable people of all time were excellent on the IQ scale. Adam, knowing both "good and evil", lost a pleasant garden and gained a muddy graveyard jungle. His descendants have waded in graveyard mud that gets deeper with every generation.

"Every day in every way, we are getting better" positive thinking sounds very reasonable *from a physical viewpoint.* Drink your milk and you will grow up to be a strong boy. "Practice dribbling a basketball enough and you can join the Globetrotters" or "Shoot enough practice shots and you will beat Curry" may work but it will not make you honest and trustworthy.

Of course, the evolutionary hypothesis is anti-God and against His words at its very roots. "God created…" as the very first Bible words, denies evolution. Some try to straddle the fence and claim a "Theistic Evolution", but fence riders are thrown up and out by God. (Revelation 3:16 KJB)

There was a time (Genesis 11) when all men spoke the same language and understood each other perfectly. But when their purpose and reason for conversant language went against God's will, God *purposely* confused their language so that one could not ask for a hammer and get one—he got slapped upside the head instead—for cursing! In Acts 2 where all spoke different languages, God enabled the speakers' tongues and the hearers' ears to speak and hear the same language. According to the Bible, God controls human language according to His will. There is no such thing as evolutionary language development from primitive grunts to grammar.

Modern translations profess to bring the archaic, undeveloped Bible words up to date. The critic's reasoning is that current language has progressed and advanced in meaning since 1611, therefore what was spoken in 1611 can not be understood today. The opposite development is true — language has deteriorated and become more confusing today than it was in the 16th Century. Just as more gun <u>laws</u> do not equal less killings, more English words do not equal better understanding.

It is also true that the English of the KJB was never spoken by people in the 16th Century; the King James Bible is Bible English. A kind of English that defines itself so that the 21st Century reader can understand the message as well as the 16th Century reader did.

CONTEXT OF A WORD'S USAGE IN THE KJB DETERMINES ITS MEANING

A maxim is repeated many times in this book: Meaning of a word is defined or explained in the context of its usage. A single word in English has many meanings. This complexity is due to several reasons, with a word's daily cultural usage being one of them. For example, in earlier times the word "fire" may have only been used as a noun to give the meaning of a material being consumed by burning, but until later, never used as a verb to describe a dismissal or "firing" of an employee. Within the field of physiology, "fire" was never used to describe the transmission of impulses between cells until 1878. Language constantly changes. *This constant change of word meanings does not always mean progress in understanding.* Some changes are helpful, but some lead to a less descriptive communication when contextual usage is ignored.

One major feature of the King James Bible translation is allowing context to determine the meaning of certain terms.

By that means it paused or stopped the so-called 'advanced evolution' of the English language.

Men call this "archaic" language, meaning old words, but old does not necessarily mean useless, non-communicative (descriptive) or less prescriptive (definitive) language. By contextual usage the KJB furnishes a stable, unchanging, descriptive as well as prescriptive dictionary and lexicon of the English language.

One reason the Bible does this is that God's message is of supreme importance to the English-speaking peoples. Since God is Holy and unchanging, His word to mankind must also be unchanging. Since God is Omniscient, His words to mankind must also be Omniscient and Omnipotent. The Holy Bible declares this to be so. A selection of His word from Psalm 119 is appropriate. This Psalm has 176 statements and every verse deals with the value and quality of God's word.

Psalm 119:9 BETH. Wherewithal shall a young man cleanse his way? by taking heed *thereto* according to thy word.

Psa 119:50 This *is* my comfort in my affliction: for thy word hath quickened me.

Psa 119:72 The law of thy mouth *is* better unto me than thousands of gold and silver.

Psa 119:73 JOD. Thy hands have made me and fashioned me: give me understanding, that I may learn thy commandments.

Psa 119:89 LAMED. For ever, O LORD, thy word is settled in heaven.

Psa 119:98 Thou through thy commandments hast made me wiser than mine enemies: for they *are* ever with me.

Psa 119:99 I have more understanding than all my teachers: for thy testimonies *are* my meditation.

Psa 119:100 I understand more than the ancients, because I keep thy precepts.

Psa 119:104 Through thy precepts I get understanding: therefore I hate every false way.

Psa 119:105 NUN. Thy word *is* a lamp unto my feet, and a light unto my path.

Psa 119:130 The entrance of thy words giveth light; it giveth understanding unto the simple.

Psa 119:137 TZADDI. Righteous *art* thou, O LORD, and upright *are* thy judgments.

Psa 119:138 Thy testimonies *that* thou hast commanded *are* righteous and very faithful.

Psa 119:144 The righteousness of thy testimonies *is* everlasting: give me understanding, and I shall live.

Psa 119:160 Thy word *is* true *from* the beginning: and every one of thy righteous judgments *endureth* for ever.

Psa 119:172 My tongue shall speak of thy word: for all thy commandments *are* righteousness.

Since God created people for His pleasure and fellowship, it is reasonable to assume He would create a people capable of understanding His will that is to be done by giving unchanging words in an unchanging Book. That Book, I believe is the Holy Bible, and that Book in the English language is the King James Bible.

Although it is the will of God that people understand His word, it is not to be assumed that when men claim to not understand it that it is due to a fault of His word. The essential truths are very clear. What English speaker cannot understand this statement?

"In the beginning God created the heaven and the earth." (Genesis 1:1 KJB)

The verse has 10 simple English words. My children at 4 years of age could read the sentence. All six understood the sentence claims there is a God and that He created the heaven and earth. All six believed from childhood the Holy scriptures.

Complexity of language or archaic words are not the problem when a man says "I cannot understand the King James Bible." The problem is not *understanding* — the problem is *belief.*

"The fool hath said in his heart, *There is* no God. They are corrupt, they have done abominable works, *there is* none that doeth good." (Psalm 14:1)

The "heart" is where a man decides to believe or reject. He decides in his heart or innermost being to not believe, his head or conscience tells him otherwise. There are no true atheists — there are only God rejecting fools.

What person cannot understand this simple sentence?

"…Believe on the Lord Jesus Christ, and thou shalt be saved…" (Acts 16:31)

The problem is not understanding, the problem is unbelief.

GOD'S BOOK WAS NEVER INTENDED TO BE AN EASY READ

The Bible was never designed to be understood like the Sunday newspaper comics. Essential truths for salvation are very easily understood, but God's eternal plans for mankind deliberately require dedicated study. In other words, if a person wants to go to Heaven first class, he must burn the midnight oil in Bible study, following God's study instructions with a daily walk in God's paths. If a person wants to ride Heaven's rails like a lazy bum, with no study and no correct walk, he can. This is a free ride but there is a cost at the station end.

There are two types of students in God's classroom:

Isaiah 28:9 Whom shall he teach knowledge? and whom shall he make to understand doctrine? *them that are* **weaned from the milk,** *and* **drawn from the breasts.**

Isaiah 28:10 For precept *must be* **upon precept, precept upon precept; line upon line, line upon line; here a little,** *and* **there a little:**

This first student understands the lessons. He understands because he humbly begins by receiving and believing the milk of God's word (basic truths) and progresses to spiritual food that requires a "chewing on it" for proper digestion. This is a step by step process, each step and line moving upward in understanding. It is not a one hour or few days study but a lifetime of learning truth.

The other type of student is a "slow learner" who never gets a full understanding:

Isaiah 28:11 For with stammering lips and another tongue will he speak to this people.

Isaiah 28:12 To whom he said, This *is* **the rest** *wherewith* **ye may cause the weary to rest; and this** *is* **the refreshing: yet they would not hear.**

Isaiah 28:13 But the word of the LORD was unto them precept upon precept, precept upon precept; line upon line, line upon line; here a little, *and* **there a little; that they might go, and fall backward, and be broken, and snared, and taken.**

The lessons that were a blessing to the first student become a snare and anything but a blessing to the second type student. God repeats the lesson over and over in many ways but they do not hear the message. The problem is not with God's words — the problem is with the ears upon whom it falls. They have ears but simply do not have the kind of ears needed. When the good seed does not grow, it is not the seed's fault, it is a problem with the ground.

When the word of God hearer does not accept or trust the words, it does not produce growth in this life. The problem is with the ground—the hearer. Instead of growth there is retardation, a brokenness, a struggle, and a life of captivity. The word of God is designed to be a curse or blessing. The word of God is a blessing to the believer and a curse to Its critic.

BIBLE NUMEROLOGY

Biblical numerology (study of numbers) is completely different from numerology used in the superstitious astrology or horoscope prognostications. Even biblical numerology is secondary and complex so that Bible doctrine should not be based upon numbers alone. In my opinion, biblical numerology is secondary to clear language discovery and can be illustrative or even entertaining in Bible study.

There are definite cultural and language influences by Bible numbers, especially in the English text and composition of the King James Bible. For example, why is the floor *number of 13* omitted in most western hospitals? Why is *File 13* known as the trash can? Why select *"Friday the Thirteenth"* as a movie title for a horror picture? Why does a man get *"40 winks"* when asleep? There are many other numerical figures that convey various numerical influences.

Various emblems and symbols of the United States of America contain the number thirteen. A repetition of certain numbers is due to Bible influence. One dominant example is that the United States of America began with thirteen colonies and, to represent that fact, there are thirteen stars on the Great Seal of the United States, thirteen stripes with the alternating colors of red and white are on the American flag.

On the principal side of the Great Seal of the United States, there are thirteen stars overhead. The shield in front of the eagle bears thirteen stripes (seven white and six red). In the eagle's right talon, is the Olive Branch of Peace, bearing thirteen olives and thirteen olive leaves. In the eagle's left talon are the Weapons of War, consisting of thirteen arrows. In the eagle's mouth is a scroll bearing the national motto "E Pluribus Unum" (thirteen letters). The Seal's reverse side is an unfinished pyramid consisting of thirteen levels of blocks. There are many symbols of freemasonry on the seal such as the pyramid and "all-seeing" eye.

The number 13 is repeated in USA symbols and documents.

Is that due to the KJB association with 13 and rebellion? The Revolutionary War of 1776 was also known as a war of rebellion of 13 colonies against England's rule. The major War of Rebellion was the Civil War of 1861 and has several connections to the number 13.

It is *interesting*, to say the least, that the USA was founded on the number 13. It is also of note that in the culture of the West—13 is considered the unlucky number. The USA with its "13" is a "melting pot" of nations and is omitted from Bible history and prophecy while the countries of Italy, Russia, Iraq, Turkey, and Israel and others are directly or indirectly mentioned in Bible history and prophecy.

Numerical study concentrates on how and where a number instance occurs in what context in the English King James Bible (AV 1611). To my knowledge, the same observations do not occur in any other translation, revision, or language of the Bible. Below is the list of Biblical numbers, categories, and a representative text of each number. The reader should be advised that the number category may well include other categories; the text list only contains the earliest biblical reference.

<u>NUMBER:</u> <u>CATEGORY:</u> <u>TEXT</u>

One: The number of God: "Hear, O Israel: The LORD our God *is* one LORD:" (Deut 6:4)

Two: Division/Testimony: "At the mouth of two witnesses, or three witnesses, shall he that is worthy of death be put to death; but at the mouth of one witness he shall not be put to death." (Deut 17:6)

Three: Confirmation/Resurrection: "After two days will he revive us: in the third day he will raise us up, and we shall live in his sight." (Hosea 6:2)

Four: Earth/Creation: "And the evening and the morning were the fourth day." (Gen 1:19) *The earth creation completed by fourth day.*

Five: Death: "And all the days that Adam lived were nine hundred and thirty years: and he died." (Gen 5:5) *(Chapter 5, verse 5 and 930 is 5x186; Christ's substitutionary death and shedding of blood, result of 5 piercings)*

Six: Man: "And the evening and the morning were the sixth day." (Gen 1:31) *(Man created on the sixth day.)*

Seven: Completion: "And on the seventh day God ended his work which he had made; and he rested on the seventh day from all his work which he had made." (Gen 2:2).. *This is a strong indication of the completeness meaning of the number 7.*

Eight: New, Superabundant: There is no actual "eighth" of Creation or time or music. The 'eighth' is the beginning again of the series 1 through 7 with some quality added.

Nine: Fruitfulness: Nine is proven by Bible text and culture—see below.

Ten: Gentile Government: Ten is proven by Bible text and culture—see below.

Eleven: Judgment: Eleven is proven by Bible text and culture—see below.

Twelve: Israel Government: Twelve is proven by Bible text and culture—see below.

Thirteen: Evil/Rebellion: Thirteen is proven by Bible text and culture—see below.

ONE: (Rev 22:13) "I am Alpha and Omega, the beginning and the end, the first and the last."

(Isa 43:10-11) "Ye *are* my witnesses, saith the LORD, and my servant whom I have chosen: that ye may know and believe me, and understand that I *am* he: before me there was no God formed, neither shall there be after me. (11) I, *even I, am* the LORD; and beside me *there is* no saviour."

The first Bible book, chapter, and verse (Genesis 1:1) declares the primacy, all sufficiency and total unity of ONE GOD.

TWO: (2 Timothy 2:15) "Study to shew thyself approved unto God, a workman that needeth not to be ashamed, rightly dividing the word of truth."

The Bible workman is admonished to "rightly divide" the word of truth in the *second* book and *second* chapter. Notice he is to "RIGHTLY" divide.

The Bible has 7 sets of books divided into at least two and form a basic definition of division; 1 and 2 Samuel, 1 and 2 Kings, 1 and 2 Chronicles, 1 and 2 Corinthians, 1 and 2 Thessalonians, 1 and 2 Timothy, 1 and 2 Peter.

In every case, the first book differs in content from that of the second book. For example: 1 Samuel; Saul is man's choice as King. 2 Samuel; David is God's choice as King. 1 Kings; David to Solomon; Israel is in the land. 2 Kings; Israel is in captivity. 1 Chronicles; Generations from Adam to David. 2 Chronicles; From Solomon to destruction of Jerusalem. 1 Corinthians; Sin in church. 2 Corinthians; Reproof of church. 1 Thessalonians; Coming for the Church. 2 Corinthians; Coming with the Church. 1 Timothy; Study of the word. 2 Timothy; Inspiration of the word. 1 Peter; To scattered church. 2 Peter; Exhortation to church.

THREE: Number of Persons in the Godhead. (Rev 1:4) "John to the seven churches which are in Asia: Grace *be* unto you, and peace, from **(a)** him which is, and which was, and which is to come; and from **(b)** the seven Spirits which are before his throne; (5) And from **(c)** Jesus Christ, *who is* the faithful witness, *and* the first begotten of the dead, and the prince of the kings of the earth. Unto him that loved us, and washed us from our sins in his own blood, (6) And hath made us kings and priests unto God and his Father; to him *be* glory and dominion for ever and ever. Amen."

Also, 3 is the number of Resurrection and Confirmation.

Galatians: 9 is the number of fruitfulness and 9 months is a normal length of pregnancy. Nine letters are in Galatians, the ninth book in NT, and is the only Bible+ book where we read of the ninefold fruit of the Spirit.

Isaiah is a little Bible within the Bible — an exact layout of OT/NT of the KJB. Isaiah was written 600+ years before even an English Bible or language existed. OT: 1-39 NT 40-66 etc. (Many Isaiah chapters correspond to books both in the OT/NT)

2 is the number of testimony/division in both OT/NT KJB. Ever noticed the 1,2 Bible books in both OT/NT? 1 Samuel, King Saul/ 2 Samuel, King David. I Thessalonians and II Thessalonians: 1 deals with Christ catching out believers from the earth, 2 deals with Christ's Second coming to earth.

Gospel of John — written to show the Deity of Jesus, has 7 days that correspond to the 7 dispensations. 14 times "I am" occurs in John (a double 7) . Isaiah 43 is where JW's claim to deny the Deity of Christ. Guess which KJB Bible book is number 43?

Book of Acts has 4 groups of 7 chapters.

Gospel of Matthew has 4 groups of 7 chapters.

6 is the number of man- Romans is 6th NT book. Joshua is 6th OT book-both have 6 letters in English. Hebrew Joshua means same as NT Jesus.

Romans has 6 verses where in English the 6th word is man. The last verse is Romans 6:6. Man was created on 6th day-we bury him 6 feet under—man works 6 days and if he is 6 ft, he is average height.

7 is tied with Israel too many times to count. Sabbath of week, of land (work land 6-rest 7th year), Sabbath of sabbaths (7 X 70 years)

Gentile number is 10.United Nations judged in Genesis 11. Israel (12 tribes). Nation of Israel begins in Genesis 12.

Never use numerology as a proof or cornerstone for doctrine—but rather use it for an attention getter in teaching. Numerology also proves our (English) cultural roots are in the KJB. Where does the number 13 bear such influence in other cultures and languages?

Teenage years are known as independence/rebellion. The first "teen" year is age thirteen. In Genesis 13 :13 read of the sin of sodomy. Genesis 14:4 records the first occurrence of the number: "In the thirteenth year they rebelled.."

In the majority of Bible chapter 13s something bad of rebellious happens. Take notice of these: File 13, Floor 13, Seat 13, Military Article 13.

13 colonies rebelled against British rule. There are 13 stars on the "REBEL" Confederate Battle flag. In Revelation 13 the antichrist shows up. In John 13:26 (the 26th chapter thirteen in the KJB) verse 26 is a double of 13. There are thirteen persons present in the 26th (2 X13) chapter 13 of the KJB, in verse 26 (2 X 13) Judas Iscariot is the thirteenth person who will betray Jesus, and his name in English has 13 letters.

The number of the antichrist is "666".

(Revelation 13:18 KJB) Here is wisdom. Let him that hath understanding count the number of the beast: for it is the number of a man; and his number *is* Six hundred threescore *and* six.

666 is a multiple of man's number, indicating a "superman" — the epitome of all mankind. He is revealed in a Bible chapter 13, and a verse 18 (6 X 6 X 6).

WHAT TIME IS IT?

The Bible is God's designed, coordinated, and chronological record of events, people, and objects. From the beginning throughout, there is a connective pattern woven in the warp and wolf of its words. Omit or change one word in the first Bible book, Genesis, and the reader may lose a related truth found in the last book, Revelation.

Time fails us to cover all the detailed union discovered in the King James Bible (KJB). The divine design and furniture of the wilderness tent — the Tabernacle — is a pattern of things in the Heavens. Genesis is related to Revelation; Joshua is connected to Romans, and the seven days numbered in the Gospel of John 1-4, correspond to the seven ages of Bible world history. The Old Testament book of Isaiah is separated from the New Testament by a writing date of almost seven centuries, but its 66 chapters give a corresponding layout to the entirety of the KJB's 66 books. Possibly one of the earliest OT books written, Job's chapters (42) illustrate a unique period of 42 desolate future months, and the conclusive doubled blessings of "the greatest of all the men of the east." Joseph's rejection by his brothers, sold into slavery for 30 pieces of silver at first, and his acceptance by them after a 7 year famine, prefigures the first and Second Coming of Christ to His fleshly brethren, Israel. Moses leaving Egypt, spending time among other peoples, and then returning to lead God's "first born" son out of Egyptian bondage by the power of a lamb's blood is mirrored by the life and work of Christ centuries later.

The OT account of Abraham's "only begotten son" Isaac, delivered from death by a substitute sacrifice, strongly prefigures the substitutionary Person and work of God's virgin born "Only Begotten Son" the Lord Jesus Christ.

Prescriptive in meaning and descriptive in its readability, the King James Bible is a perfect blend of OT shadows and types to the NT antitypes and provides sense and understanding to the conscientious Bible believer.

The King James Bible, (the cumulative and final effort of seven English translations from c. 1400-1600 AD) is the purified (Psalm 12:6) English translation of an Oriental book, with English as a relative newcomer among world languages, tells God's history of His dealings with one people, Israel, as no other book. It is hard to miss the significance of God's creation of the universe taking only 11 short chapters, and then spending the rest of the Bible's 1,178 chapters relating the promises, blessings, successes, and failures of one nation — Israel.

The cause and finality of God's future earthly dealings with the nation of Israel is this study's concern. This future period is known by several terms in the KJB: "the time of Jacob's trouble" (Jeremiah 30:7), "great tribulation" (Matthew 24:21), "one week" (Daniel 9:27), "great day of the LORD", (Zephaniah 1:14) "day of wrath", "day of trouble and distress", "day of wasteness and desolation", "day of darkness and gloominess" (Zephaniah 1:15). A "day" in the KJB may be a short period of c. 12 hours of solar light, an evening and morning of approximately 24 hours, or a longer period of time determined by the context.

"Day" is used to designate various time periods in the final Bible book, Revelation. In Revelation 1:10 John says, **"I was in the Spirit on the Lord's day, and heard behind me a great voice, as of a trumpet,"** That "day" will be one thousand and seven years of 24 hour periods and reach into eternity. Revelation 4:8 and 7:15 is a 12 hour period of light. Revelation 6:17 is a day of seven years. Revelation 8:12 "day" is 4 hours. Revelation 9:15;12:10;14:11;16:14;18:8 "day" is a 24 hour period. Revelation 20:10 and 21:25 "day" is eternal.

It may be beneficial to make a right division point of Bible doctrine at this point. The KJB is understood by proper division. As a surgeon understands the different functions and locations of organs in a human body by a course named "Gross Anatomy"-- which course consists of cutting and separating the various body parts, so a Bible student learns the purpose and functions of the various ages of the whole body of doctrine in the Bible.

"Study to shew thyself approved unto God, a workman that needeth not to be ashamed, rightly dividing the word of truth." (2 Timothy 2:15 KJB)

At the present time of this lesson (2022) we are between the cross and catching out of the Church, which is the Body of Christ. The present age (also known as a "dispensation") is named "the day of salvation." This present age or "day of Salvation" is not the same as the future "day of the Lord".

"(For he saith, I have heard thee in a time accepted, and in the day of salvation have I succoured thee: behold, now is the accepted time; behold, now is the day of salvation.) (2 Corinthians 6:2 KJB)"

We (the Body of Christ) are promised that in no wise will we ever be under the wrath of God. The Body of Christ will be caught out of the earth to meet the Lord Jesus at the end of this day of salvation (1 Thessalonians 4:13-18) and <u>BEFORE</u> the day of the Lord's wrath comes in the book of Revelation.

"But God commendeth his love toward us, in that, while we were yet sinners, Christ died for us. 9 Much more then, being now justified by his blood, we shall be saved from wrath through him." (Romans 5:8-9 KJB)

"For they themselves shew of us what manner of entering in we had unto you, and how ye turned to God from idols to serve the living and true God; 10 And to wait for his Son from heaven, whom he raised from the dead, even Jesus, which delivered us from the wrath to come." (1 Thessalonians 1:9-10 KJB)
"For God hath not appointed us to wrath, but to obtain salvation by our Lord Jesus Christ," (1 Thessalonians 5:9 KJB)

The Book of "The Revelation of Jesus Christ" (Revelation 1:1) the angel gave to the apostle John is not an allegoristic or apocryphal story, nor is the book events to be treated as non-literal or with some spiritualistic interpretation, the detailed specificity of the events and time periods of these days accentuate the literal reality of the events.

Failure to allow the KJB to "say what it means and mean what it says" in Revelation usually begins with careless reading of the first verse:

(Revelation 1:1 KJB) "The Revelation of Jesus Christ, which God gave unto him, to shew unto his servants things which must shortly come to pass; and he sent and signified *it* by his angel unto his servant John:

Believing exactly what the verse says: the First Person (The Father) of the Godhead (not the first God) gave to the Second Person (The Son) of the Godhead (not the second God) information the Second Person did not have in His earthly ministry (virgin birth to His bodily resurrection and ascension back into Heaven).

This was sent by "signified" Revelation (a book full of visible signs) from the Father for the Angel of the LORD to deliver the book to the Apostle John so that the servants of the Lord might know the things which would shortly (not in the immediate first century time, but shortly or quickly happen in relation to where and when John was located to receive the Revelation—not "shortly" to his location and time (possibly Sunday or the first day of a week) on the Isle of Patmos—but to the future occurrence of the prophesied time of the OT day of the LORD or NT the Lord's day. Both OT and NT "day" are reference to the same period.

This is because OT was originally written in Hebrew and the NT written in Greek. Greek has normal descriptive adjectives whereas Hebrew must use two or more nouns in a prepositional phrase to describe a noun.

If the reader of the above paragraph does not believe the Trinitarian Godhead (Three equal Persons in One Godhead) or why the Lord Jesus, without compromising His Deity, limited Himself in the knowledge of when His Second Coming to Israel would be, or how John was moved prophetically to observe and write of a future period of time known as "the Lord's day" (as the prophet Ezekiel was moved in time)---if the reader does not believe these three things, it will be impossible for him to believe the rest of the Book of the Revelation, and thus remain ignorant of "things to come."

Figurative language is a part of normal-literal interpretation. Where a figure of speech is used, it represents reality; the figure or symbol is explained. For example:

"The mystery of the seven stars which thou sawest in my right hand, and the seven golden candlesticks. The seven stars are the angels of the seven churches: and the seven candlesticks which thou sawest are the seven churches." (Revelation 1:20 KJB)

Once a Bible mystery is defined or explained, it is no longer a mystery. Some pundit gave a simple rule: to discover a figure of speech, first try to read it as literal. If the literal meaning makes sense, seek no other sense, lest you get nonsense.

The false but popular allegorical interpretation of the seven churches in Revelation 2-3 as periods of church age history encourages unbelief and confuses "Revelation" (Greek: ἀποκάλυψις: manifest, open, revealed, removal or unveiling) with (ἀπόκρυφος) a word that means "hidden" or "unknown" meanings: *Apocalypse with Apocrypha*. Some interpreters actually make the Book of Revelation a book of hidden and unknown meanings or meanings that exist in the imagination of whomever is doing the interpretation. Is it too much to expect the term "churches" means "churches" and not 'periods of history'??

Treating the churches as church age periods requires further speculation and unbelief of all the book. The Book of Revelation is written directly to all seven FUTURE churches of Asia (Revelation 1:4, 11, 20; 22:16) with specific remarks to each local church: Ephesus (2:1-7), Smyrna (2:8-11), Pergamos (2:12-17), Thyatira (2:18-28), Sardis (3:1-6), Philadelphia (3:7-13), Laodicea (3:14-21). The Revelation is "for" all our learning, but all is not directed for us to follow or do.

The seven churches are not scores of scattered churches throughout decades of time with members in the Church which is the one body of Christ. No one in Revelation **is baptized by the Spirit into the Body of Christ (1 Corinthians 12:13); no one has** security of salvation (Romans 8:28). They are local organizations, not organisms and all are under the leadership of an angel, not a pastor, bishop, or elder! Furthermore, their relationship to the Lord is not secure. They are in His hand, not a member of His hand, and temporarily in His mouth—not a member of His Body (Romans 12:5) and liable (if they don't 'overcome' by their works) to being spewed out.

The Book of Daniel is the "calendar" book in the KJB. God gives four specific time periods and identifies the start and end of each period by an event.

It may seem to us mortals that making an issue of how you treat a gift of land is a little "nit-picky" but it does nothing but demonstrate a Bible truth: **"For my thoughts are not your thoughts, neither are your ways my ways, saith the LORD. 9 For as the heavens are higher than the earth, so are my ways higher than your ways, and my thoughts than your thoughts." (Isaiah 55:8-9 KJB)**

Believe it or not, the Book of Daniel explains a great part of the reason God's wrath is poured out in the book of Revelation. It is true that "the whole world lieth in wickedness" because of the devil (1 John 5:19) but that is not the reason for the wrath of God. It is also true that "all have sinned and come short of the glory of God" (Romans 3:23). And there is no doubt that we as all men have "walked according to the course of this world, according to the prince of the power of the air, the spirit that now worketh in the children of disobedience: 3 Among whom also we all had our conversation in times past in the lusts of our flesh, fulfilling the desires of the flesh and of the mind; and were by nature the children of wrath, even as others. " (Ephesians 2:2-3) But that is not the main reason for God's Day of wrath!

The reason lies outside my knowledge. Did the failure to keep the land sabbath only contribute to the reason for the *length* (seven years) of the "Tribulation"? I honestly do not know, neither have I read that others know. It is scripturally reasonable to account Israel's rejection and crucifixion of Jesus a great portion of the fact for the wrath of God but the time requirement is a puzzle.

Regardless, Daniel learned the time frame from the angel Gabriel.

Daniel 9:21 Yea, whiles I *was* speaking in prayer, even the man Gabriel, whom I had seen in the vision at the beginning, being caused to fly swiftly, touched me about

the time of the evening oblation.

9:22 And he informed *me,* and talked with me, and said, O Daniel, I am now come forth to give thee skill and understanding.

9:23 At the beginning of thy supplications the commandment came forth, and I am come to shew *thee;* for thou *art* greatly beloved: therefore understand the matter, and consider the vision.

9:24 Seventy weeks are determined upon thy people and upon thy holy city, to finish the transgression, and to make an end of sins, and to make reconciliation for iniquity, and to bring in everlasting righteousness, and to seal up the vision and prophecy, and to anoint the most Holy.

9:25 Know therefore and understand, *that* from the going forth of the commandment to restore and to build Jerusalem unto the Messiah the Prince *shall be* seven weeks, and threescore and two weeks: the street shall be built again, and the wall, even in troublous times.

9:26 And after threescore and two weeks shall Messiah be cut off, but not for himself: and the people of the prince that shall come shall destroy the city and the sanctuary; and the end thereof *shall be* with a flood, and unto the end of the war desolations are determined.

9:27 And he shall confirm the covenant with many for one week: and in the midst of the week he shall cause the sacrifice and the oblation to cease, and for the overspreading of abominations he shall make *it* desolate, even until the consummation, and that determined shall be poured upon the desolate.

The layout of time was understood by Daniel from his study of the prophet Jeremiah and the further details explained by Gabriel.

DANIEL'S SEVENTY

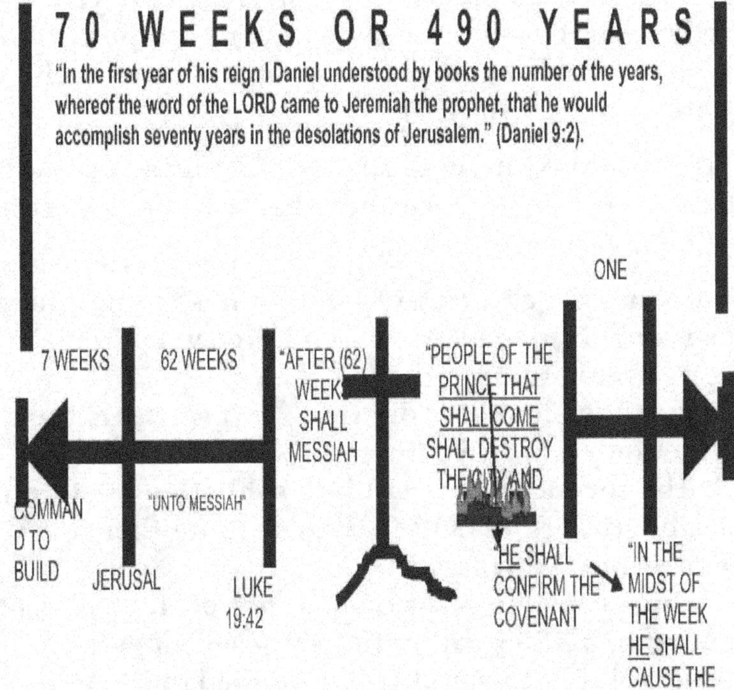

The Jeremiah passages that have to do with Daniel's 70 Weeks are those where you see the number "seventy" and "seven". Daniel was also aware of Moses prophetic warnings in the Law regarding land.

"11 And this whole land shall be a desolation, *and* an astonishment; and these nations shall serve the king of Babylon seventy years.

12 And it shall come to pass, when seventy years are accomplished, *that* I will punish the king of Babylon, and that nation, saith the LORD, for their iniquity, and the land of the Chaldeans, and will make it perpetual desolations." (Jeremiah 25:11-12 KJB)

"10 For thus saith the LORD, That after seventy years be accomplished at Babylon I will visit you, and perform my good word toward you, in causing you to return to this place." (Jeremiah 29:10 KJB)

We can look in Leviticus for a "7 times" that has to do with Israel's problems when they disobey God regarding the land sabbath-there are several:

"2 Speak unto the children of Israel, and say unto them, When ye come into the land which I give you, then shall the land keep a sabbath unto the LORD.
3 Six years thou shalt sow thy field, and six years thou shalt prune thy vineyard, and gather in the fruit thereof;
4 But in the seventh year shall be a sabbath of rest unto the land, a sabbath for the LORD: thou shalt neither sow thy field, nor prune thy vineyard.
5 That which groweth of its own accord of thy harvest thou shalt not reap, neither gather the grapes of thy vine undressed: *for* it is a year of rest unto the land.
6 And the sabbath of the land shall be meat for you; for thee, and for thy servant, and for thy maid, and for thy hired servant, and for thy stranger that sojourneth with thee,
7 And for thy cattle, and for the beast that *are* in thy land, shall all the increase thereof be meat.
8 And thou shalt number seven sabbaths of years unto thee, seven times seven years; and the space of the seven sabbaths of years shall be unto thee forty and nine years.
9 Then shalt thou cause the trumpet of the jubile to sound on the tenth *day* of the seventh month, in the day of atonement shall ye make the trumpet sound throughout all your land." (Leviticus 25:2-9 KJB)

"And if ye will not yet for all this hearken unto me, then I will punish you seven times more for your sins." (Leviticus 26:18 KJB)

This is the most important passage in understanding the "why" of Daniel's Seventy Weeks. Israel not only had a <u>weekly sabbath of days</u> (work for six days and rest the seventh) she had a <u>land sabbath</u> where the land was to be worked six years and *then "rested" the seventh year*. Many of those who speak so loud regarding the "sabbath day" never mention the land sabbath! Israel also had a "sabbath of sabbaths" every fifty years. The land sabbath is the very reason for the 70 Weeks (sevens) of years exacted upon Israel. (See Jacob working a "week" or 7 years for a wife: Genesis 27:28-29).

Israel did not keep 70 of the land sabbaths and when God "collects" them, He takes them back in 7 times 70 prophetic years. He stopped the clock before the last week of the 70 is collected. From the commandment to build the walls and city unto Messiah the Prince was 69 weeks of years: land sabbaths. Israel was not allowed to have the land God had promised to Abraham and his seed.

The land promise along with the other promises of Genesis 12 must be kept; the Abrahamic Covenant was unconditional but God did not exclude punishment for disobedience of the nation. God stopped the clock that collected the land sabbaths at the end of the 69th week. The land will not be enjoyed by Israel until the last week is paid: the 70th week in which Israel will have Great Tribulation, the culmination being "the time of Jacob's trouble." And only then will the nation return to God and He will return to them and put them in the promised land.

"And I will scatter you among the heathen, and will draw out a sword after you: and your land shall be desolate, and your cities waste. 34 Then shall the land enjoy her sabbaths, as long as it lieth desolate, and ye *be* in your enemies' land; *even* then shall the land rest, and enjoy her sabbaths. 35 As long as it lieth desolate it shall rest; because it did not rest in your sabbaths, when ye dwelt upon it." (Leviticus 26:33-35 KJB)**

Israel was given a merciful opportunity to receive the promises during the earthly ministry of Christ and also during the early part of Acts. (Acts 2-8). The nation rejected Christ and then blasphemed the Holy Ghost in the apostles' ministry (Acts 7:51) and the clock remained silent. Now, the 70th week must be collected in the future.

"And if ye walk contrary unto me, and will not hearken unto me; I will bring seven times more plagues upon you according to your sins." (Leviticus 26:21 KJB)

Certain words used by Peter in Acts 2 and 3 are also critical:

1. Restitution: The Bible definition of _restitution_ is payment for something misused, whether it is defined in the Hebrew, Greek or English. Restitution under the Law of Moses demands the return or compensation to the owner of that which was lost, stolen, abused, or damaged.

2. Refreshing: a definition of re-freshing is a renewal of a prior damaged condition.

"If the sun be risen upon him, there shall be blood shed for him; for he should make full restitution; if he have nothing, then he shall be sold for his theft." (Exodus 22:3 KJB. Also see Exodus 22:6, 12)

The meaning of restitution is very important in prophetic studies, especially in the context of its usage. Look at Acts 3 and what Peter says:

"Repent ye therefore, and be converted, that your sins may be blotted out, when the times of refreshing shall come from the presence of the Lord; 20 And he shall send Jesus Christ, which before was preached unto you: 21 Whom the heaven must receive until the times of restitution of all things, which God hath spoken by the mouth of all his holy prophets since the world began." (Acts 3:19-21 KJB)

In Acts 2 and 3 Peter knew nothing about the immediate spiritual blessings of the cross. In Acts 2 and 3 he is preaching to the men of the nation of Israel (Acts 3:12) who agreed with their leaders in rejection and crucifixion of Christ.

When did Peter in Acts 2 say Israel's sins would be blotted out? Answer: "when the times of refreshing come from the presence of the Lord". Where was Jesus at the time of Peter's statement? Answer: In Heaven. Peter did not know what Paul knew — sins were blotted out at the cross for a special body of people : **"For as many of you as have been baptized into Christ have put on Christ. 28 There is neither Jew nor Greek, there is neither bond nor free, there is neither male nor female: for ye are all one in Christ Jesus." (Galatians 3:27-28 KJB)** *The baptism "into Christ" is not a baptism into water by a man — it is the baptism by the Spirit into Christ spoken of by Paul in 1 Corinthians 12:13!*

"And you, being dead in your sins and the uncircumcision of your flesh, hath he quickened together with him, having forgiven you all trespasses; 14 Blotting out the handwriting of ordinances that was against us, which was contrary to us, and took it out of the way, nailing it to his cross;" (Colossians 2:13-14 KJB)

Both Peter and Paul are correct — if you see that Peter refers to Israel in a future age (the day of the Lord when the Lord returns to Israel in Revelation 19) and that Paul in

Colossians refers to the present age, the day of salvation in which the present body of Christ is composed of all men, and members are counted neither Jew nor Greek).

Jesus, after His crucifixion and resurrection ascended back into heaven with the promise that He will return to the earth.

John 14:3 And if I go and prepare a place for you, I will come again, and receive you unto myself; that where I am, *there* ye may be also.

Although Jesus knew what was to happen between His departure from the earth and second coming again to the earth — He did not reveal the events or sequences or results, simply because the disciples did not need to know when John 14 was spoken. They did not know at that time He would be rejected and crucified. It is very important for the Bible student to get the correct sequence of events and the people who are involved with those events. Otherwise, understanding of all Bible prophecy will be confused and misappropriated.

Peter did not know that an unknown, time period, undesignated, when an unexpected long or short period of time would occur between the Lord's ascension into Heaven and His return to earth.

Peter also did not know all the spiritual blessings that would result to all the nations of the death, burial, and resurrection of Christ because that was not revealed until God gave the revelation to Paul. Peter did not know many things but Peter did know the correct order of events of what had been revealed in the Lord's past teaching (Luke 18: 31-34) and the scores of prophecies through the Old Testament prophets.

Peter deals with FUTURE events for Israel when Jesus returns to earth.

He knows nothing about what will happen until Jesus returns — he only knows the Israel has committed a great sin in rejecting their King and and the most important issue first: **<u>Israel's sins will be blotted out</u>**. This remission of sins will occur "when the times of refreshing come". Of importance to notice, is that this blotting out or remission, a total removal of sins, can not happen BEFORE (*until*) Jesus returns to the earth. These "times of refreshing" will not happen without the Lord's first returning to *Israel.*

So we see TWO "times" spoken of in Acts 3:19-21: one of "refreshing" and one of "restitution" (payment for wrong done): one of blessing and one that demands a payment to be made BEFORE the blessing. Correct prophetic interpretation of the Bible depends upon believing both will literally occur. But, correct interpretation demands that each of these "times" be properly defined by Bible usage and context.

"Which also said, Ye men of Galilee, why stand ye gazing up into heaven? this same Jesus, which is taken up from you into heaven, shall so come in like manner as ye have seen him go into heaven." (Acts 1:11 KJB)

Peter tells the men of Israel that God the Father will "send Jesus Christ which before was preached unto you: whom heaven must receive until the times of restitution of all things." Does this mean the Jesus Christ will come BEFORE "the times of restitution"? No, a thousand times, "No!" Some try to make the return of Jesus be BEFORE, simply because they only see the preposition "until". The preposition does not control a sentence--context does.

The return of Christ is based upon first the "restitution of all things". A preposition is first defined by context. Without the noun, subject, verb, object or context of the prepositional phrase, the meaning is meaningless. And, if the object of the preposition is mangled by ignorance of the object's definition, confusion and error is the result.

By the use of "restitution" (a demand of repayment) Peter could never mean "Jesus will come BEFORE the restitution of all things owed." God is not making restitution to Israel of that which He owes them! Israel must make restitution to God BEFORE Jesus will return and bless them. The sentence simply means that Jesus returns to Israel AFTER Israel pays what is due.

What comprises Israel's restitution? What does Israel owe? For sure they must repent of their wickedness in rejecting Christ, that is evident. But the recompense extends beyond the crucifixion of Christ and has to do with all of God's promises to bless Israel, especially the unconditional promise to Abraham (Genesis 12:1-3) of a land for the nation, made before the Law of Moses. It all goes back to God establishing Israel as a great nation in His sight and giving them a piece of His land on this earth.

All the world's trouble in the book of revelation center around Israel and are related to Israel. The church which is the body of Christ is not mentioned one time. Nothing is revealed in Revelation that is not already prophesied in the Old Testament. It is a revelation of when things happen, it is not a revelation of OT meanings. All persons, angels, objects, and battles in Revelation are identified in the Old Testament.

FACEBOOK BIBLIOLOGY

A 2022 Facebook contributor offered this view in criticism of King James Bible believers. We avoid identification of him in hope he will learn beyond this level.

"KJVO inerrantists who claim to believe God preserved his inerrant word in the AV1611 but cannot point to an inerrant Bible prior to 1611 are logically inconsistent.
They cannot point to one because there are none that agree with the KJV in its entirety.
KJVOs it's time to rethink your doctrine of preservation and get on board with orthodoxy."
("KJVO" is his acronym for "King James Version Only")

These theological whiz kids may justly be called "shadetree theologians" or "sandbox Bible experts" because of their amateurish arguments and use of some mangled apologetics. The "KJVO" accusation is what he ignorantly attempts to define— Bible believers have NEVER said the inspired or inerrant Bible words were not in existence before 1611. "Inspiration" is present tense and given by God—it is not by some man's hand in the past on a piece of leather, papyrus, or paper. The result of the scripture statement, "All scripture is given by inspiration of God" is inerrancy. The argument about not finding "an inerrant Bible prior to 1611" is childish.

What this "expert" has done is he has painted himself into a corner. He does not believe any Bible is 100% accurate or the inerrant word of God. His "orthodoxy" is actually heresy. If he claims to believe that *only* the original Bible manuscripts were inspired, his belief is based upon what is nonexistent. His "faith" would be impugned and laughed out of every courtroom in the world.

Historical progress of written document facts and the *accuracy* of the document's facts are separate and different arguments. For example: The prior existence of a written document with all medical truth in its contents is not required to validate the latter truth of Sir William Harvey's 1628 blood circulatory discovery.

This amateur must not know that the Hebrew Masoretic text of the OT was complete and accurate centuries prior to 1611, AND that the Hebrew OT, although accurate in Hebrew, cannot be translated word for word into any other language (including English) simply because all languages have different rules for meaning, grammar and syntax.

As far as finding the NT in English/Greek/Spanish/French/Latin or any language in past history — all would be hard pressed to find an "inerrant Bible" ("Bible" implies 66 books) simply because the NT was not written before the first century AD. And, added to all that is this 'expert' cannot read with understanding the English language of 1200 AD simply because old/middle/ or modern English did not exist prior to 1200 AD.

In addition, he and his pals are hung up on inspiration being on writing material (original mss only) instead of the power of God throughout history. The Bible Timothy's grandmother and mother had in the 1st Century was given by inspiration of God.

(2 Timothy 1:5; 3:14-16 KJB) "When I call to remembrance the unfeigned faith that is in thee, which dwelt first in thy grandmother Lois, and thy mother Eunice; and I am persuaded that in thee also."

3:14 But continue thou in the things which thou hast learned and hast been assured of, knowing of whom thou hast learned *them;*

3:15 And that from a child thou hast known the holy scriptures, which are able to make thee wise unto salvation through faith which is in Christ Jesus.

3:16 All scripture *is* given by inspiration of God, and *is* profitable for doctrine, for reproof, for correction, for instruction in righteousness:

Using one of another KJB critic's own arguments — *This KJB critic ADDED one word to the Psalm 119:89 "settled __only__ in heaven".*

Psalm 119:89 LAMED. For ever, O LORD, thy word is settled in heaven.

If the word of God is settled **ONLY** IN HEAVEN, what language (s) was it in Heaven in 300 BC? Did that "Heavenly Bible" include only Genesis or all 66 books of the Bible? Of what use is a Bible in Heaven to a sinner on earth?

Our simple answer to such simpletons' questions is in kind: "Where was the inerrant Bible before 1611?" Answer: "The same place your face was before you washed it."

Romans 10:17 So then faith *cometh* by hearing, and hearing by the word of God.
Deuteronomy 32:20 And he said, I will hide my face from them, I will see what their end *shall be:* for they *are* a very froward generation, children in whom *is* no faith.

The quality of a person's faith is in direct proportion to his appraisal of the quality of the word of God in his hand.

WATER FACTS AND THE KING JAMES BIBLE

All water on earth is connected. Tap water from a USA faucet in the small southern town of Slapout, Alabama is connected to the water of the Red Sea. Bodies of water named "Atlantic Ocean" "Pacific Ocean" "Great Salt Lake" "Indian Ocean" and "Artic Ocean", etc., only specify *geographic* locations of portions of the united Earth Sea. All of the water on the Earth is constantly moving in one loop known as the "water cycle." The water cycle employs at least 6 physical processes to connect all water: evaporation, condensation, precipitation, infiltration, surface runoff, and subsurface flow.

Bernard Palissy (1510-1589) a Protestant clergy and scientist, is generally credited with discovering the process of the water cycle. The King James Bible knew this process over 6,000 years ago. Before man ever traveled over 100 miles from one side of the Earth, God's Book knew all water 2500 miles away was connected to the local well.

(Genesis 1:9-10 KJB) And God said, Let the waters under the heaven be gathered together unto one place, and let the dry *land* appear: and it was so.

10 And God called the dry *land* Earth; and the gathering together of the waters called he Seas: and God saw that *it was* good.

The word "ocean" does not appear in the word of God, Earth's water is designated by "seas". Ecclesiastes and Job, both ancient Bible books have recorded the water cycle.

(Ecclesiastes 1:7 KJB) All the rivers run into the sea; yet the sea *is* not full; unto the place from whence the rivers come, thither they return again.

(Job 36:27-28 KJB) For he maketh small the drops of water: they pour down rain according to the vapour thereof:

28 Which the clouds do drop *and* distil upon man abundantly.

Water is used as a figure of speech to signify the cleansing of one's way by obedience to the word of God.

(Ephesians 5:26 KJB) That he might sanctify and cleanse it with

the washing of water by the word,

(Psalm 119:9 KJB) BETH. Wherewithal shall a young man cleanse his way? by taking heed *thereto* according to thy word.

An average human body is 60% water although water is as much as 75% of some people! As a general rule of thumb, a human can only live about 3-5 days without water. Is it any wonder then that the word of God is likened to water?

FROM WHENCE DID THE WATER OF CREATION ORIGINATE?

Water could have been included within the greater term, "heaven and earth" of Genesis 1, but it is salient that waters creation is not specified. Waters show up but are treated as though an eternal entity.

(Genesis 1:2 KJB) And the earth was without form, and void; and darkness *was* upon the face of the deep. And the Spirit of God moved upon the face of the waters.

(Genesis 8:2 KJB) The fountains also of the deep and the windows of heaven were stopped, and the rain from heaven was restrained;

Genesis 8:2 relates, "deep" "windows of heaven" and "rain". This progressive relationship leaves no doubt that "deep" can refer to a place or places where water in some state exists. Waters existed, but no mention is made of its creation. Could this be a Divine implication, symbolic of the Eternal word of God?

(Genesis 1:3 KJB) And God said, Let there be light: and there was light.

The Spirit of God moves upon the face of the deep and is followed by the polysyndeton connective "And": "AND GOD SAID…" The creation of light and a firmament is by the word of God but no mention of a creation of waters.

The gospel account of Jesus' conversation with the Samaritan woman at the well connects physical and material water with the eternal, living, and sustaining water.

(John 4:9-14 KJB) Then saith the woman of Samaria unto him, How is it that thou, being a Jew, askest drink of me, which am a

woman of Samaria? For the Jews have no dealings with the Samaritans.

10 Jesus answered and said unto her, If thou knewest the gift of God, and who it is that saith to thee, Give me to drink; thou wouldest have asked of him, and he would have given thee living water.

11 The woman saith unto him, Sir, thou hast nothing to draw with, and the well is deep: from whence then hast thou that living water?

12 Art thou greater than our father Jacob, which gave us the well, and drank thereof himself, and his children, and his cattle?

13 Jesus answered and said unto her, Whosoever drinketh of this water shall thirst again:

14 But whosoever drinketh of the water that I shall give him shall never thirst; but the water that I shall give him shall be in him a well of water springing up into everlasting life.

The scribe Ezra "…read in the book in the law of God distinctly, and gave the sense, and caused *them* to understand the reading" at the water gate (Nehemiah 8:1,8). The selection of the city water gate (above all other city gates) as the place to expound the word of God to the people was intentional.

THE PRETRIBULATIONAL RAPTURE OF THE BODY OF CHRIST

The term "rapture"[1] does not occur in the Bible. Like many terms, this is a term of convenience to describe a doctrine. The rapture is what happens to the Church at the end of the age.

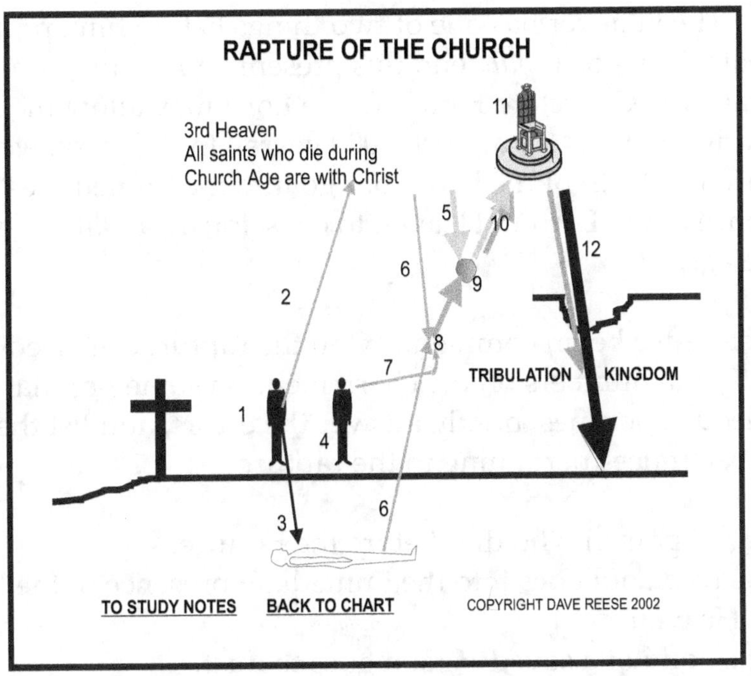

---

[1] Rapture in theology means "the act of conveying a person from one place to another."

The rapture of the Church[2] is a sign-less event. There are no specific prophecies to signal it. All attempts to set a date or pinpoint events just prior to it are guesswork at the best. There are many signs (definite prophecies of time periods, individuals, countries) related to the Coming of Christ to set up His Kingdom on earth *after* the rapture and Tribulation, but all attempts to date the rapture end in dismal failure.

The believer has one of two things before him: rapture or death. The Lord *could* end this present age at any moment and take the Church to Himself. The Lord may allow the age to continue (it has for almost 2,000 years). In that case, we experience death of the body, but go into the immediate presence of the Lord in Heaven to consciously await the end of the age.

Before we begin commentary on the rapture, we need to identify the numbers on the chart, mention some popular but erroneous doctrines, briefly answer the errors, and list the Bible references pertaining to the rapture.

1. Saved person who dies before the rapture.
2. A saved soul goes into the immediate presence of the Lord in Heaven.
3. The body of a saved person goes to dust.
4. Saved person who is living at time of rapture. He does not experience death.
5. Coming of the Lord from Heaven.
6. Soul of saved person who died before rapture is reunited with his resurrected and glorified body.
7. Living believer is changed and glorified.

---

[2] "Church" as it is used in this study refers to the Body of Christ, those who are saved in this present age that extends from the first century until the rapture (meeting the Lord in the air) occurs.

8. All people of the Church meet in the air before going to see the Lord.
9. Paul presents the Church to the Lord Jesus Christ.
10. The Church goes with the Lord to Heaven.
11. The *work* (singular) of each believer is tried and rewards given.
12. The Lord (accompanied by the Church) comes to the earth to set up His Millennial Kingdom.

We do not believe some popular doctrines have any ground in scripture. Here are a few:

1. There are signs of the rapture such as the Mark of the Beast, governments, conditions of morality, revival of Christianity, etc.
2. The Church will go through some portion of the Tribulation Period.
3. A person must be saved from each tribe or people group before the rapture can occur.
4. Doctrine related to the Church is *based* on any portion of scripture one may choose.
5. The time of the rapture may be determined by observing Israel.
6. If you are not "living for the Lord" you will miss the rapture.
7. The world will be shocked and spiritually awakened by the absence of the Church.
8. The purpose of the Judgment Seat of Christ is to see whether a person is worthy of entering Heaven.
9. The Judgment Seat of Christ is to deal with sins committed before or after salvation.
10. Unconfessed sins are dealt with at the Judgment Seat of Christ.
11. Believers living at the rapture must die before they go to Heaven.
12. Only a preacher's or teacher's work is dealt with at the Judgment Seat of Christ.

13. The errors of Partial Rapture, Mid-tribulation Rapture, and Post-tribulation Rapture are dealt with in a later section.

Almost every error above can be traced to failure to rightly dividing the word. When Israel's promises are given to the Church, or when the Church is read into passages in Matthew through John, or when Acts is not recognized as a book of transition, doctrine is misappropriated.

Brief Answers to Errors 1-12.
Details are given in the commentary below, but a short answer is given here to each one.
1. There are signs of the rapture such as the Mark of the Beast, governments, conditions of morality, revival of Christianity, etc.

Signs are for the Jew. The Church is not divided into Jew, Gentile, etc.

For the Jews require a sign, and the Greeks seek after wisdom:
(1 Corinthians 1:22).

27 For as many of you as have been baptized into Christ have put on Christ.
28 There is neither Jew nor Greek, there is neither bond nor free, there is neither male nor female: for ye are all one in Christ Jesus.
(Galatians 3:27-28).

2. The Church will go through some portion of the Tribulation Period.

This is gleaned from reading passages given to Israel regarding the tribulation, "the time of Jacob's trouble," or confusing the churches of the Book of Revelation with the Body of Christ. God has delivered us from the wrath to come. The Church has a blessed hope, not a fearful looking for the tribulation period. We are told to comfort each other concerning the rapture.

Much more then, being now justified by his blood, we shall be saved from wrath through him. (Romans 5:9).

9 For they themselves shew of us what manner of entering in we had unto you, and how ye turned to God from idols to serve the living and true God;
10 And to wait for his Son from heaven, whom he raised from the dead, even Jesus, which delivered us from the wrath to come.
(1Thessalonians 1:9-10).

Looking for that blessed hope, and the glorious appearing of the great God and our Saviour Jesus Christ; (Titus 2:13).

16 For the Lord himself shall descend from heaven with a shout, with the voice of the archangel, and with the trump of God: and the dead in Christ shall rise first:
17 Then we which are alive and remain shall be caught up together with them in the clouds, to meet the Lord in the air: and so shall we ever be with the Lord.
18 Wherefore comfort one another with these words.
(1Thessalonians 4:16-18).

3. A person must be saved from each tribe or people group before the rapture can occur.
The saints from other ages and the tribulation around the throne in the Book of Revelation are confused with the Body of Christ.

There is nothing to indicate the gospel of the grace of God is carried to each generation beyond the first century. This doctrine puts a condition on the rapture, namely, the obedience of the Church to world evangelization. On the contrary, in practice and doctrine the Church is a failure in this task. The gospel "of the kingdom" (Matthew 24) is confused with the gospel "of the grace of God."

And this gospel of the kingdom shall be preached in all the world for a witness unto all nations; and then shall the end come.
(Matthew 24:14).

The above is spoken to disciples who knew nothing about the key elements of the gospel of the grace of God: the substitutionary death, burial, and resurrection of Christ. It has to do with the Lord coming to set up His kingdom.

Those around the throne in the passage below are said to have come out "of great tribulation." They are the fruits of the preaching of the 144,000 male Jewish virgins during the tribulation period.

9 After this I beheld, and, lo, a great multitude, which no man could number, of all nations, and kindreds, and people, and tongues, stood before the throne, and before the Lamb, clothed with white robes, and palms in their hands;
10 And cried with a loud voice, saying, Salvation to our God which sitteth upon the throne, and unto the Lamb.
11 And all the angels stood round about the throne, and about the elders and the four beasts, and fell before the throne on their faces, and worshipped God,
12 Saying, Amen: Blessing, and glory, and wisdom, and thanksgiving, and honour, and power, and might, be unto our God for ever and ever. Amen.

13 And one of the elders answered, saying unto me, What are these which are arrayed in white robes? and whence came they?
14 And I said unto him, Sir, thou knowest. And he said to me, These are they which came out of great tribulation, and have washed their robes, and made them white in the blood of the Lamb.
(Revelation 7:9-14).

4. Doctrine related to the Church is *based* on any portion of scripture one may choose.

Every passage in the Bible has historical, doctrinal, and practical applications. Failure to get them straight produces devotionalized teaching that can say anything the mind of the interpreter wishes to say.

5. The time of the rapture may be determined by observing Israel.

Israel, as a nation, is cut off from blessings during this present age. They furnish no signs or blessings to the Church.

For I would not, brethren, that ye should be ignorant of this mystery, lest ye should be wise in your own conceits; that blindness in part is happened to Israel, until the fulness of the Gentiles be come in.
(Romans 11:25).

4 Though I might also have confidence in the flesh. If any other man thinketh that he hath whereof he might trust in the flesh, I more:

5 Circumcised the eighth day, of the stock of Israel, of the tribe of Benjamin, an Hebrew of the Hebrews; as touching the law, a Pharisee;

6 Concerning zeal, persecuting the church; touching the righteousness which is in the law, blameless.
7 But what things were gain to me, those I counted loss for Christ.
8 Yea doubtless, and I count all things but loss for the excellency of the knowledge of Christ Jesus my Lord: for whom I have suffered the loss of all things, and do count them but dung, that I may win Christ,
(Philippians 3:4-8).

6. If you are not "living for the Lord" you will miss the rapture.

The context below is spiritual alertness. Whether "we wake or sleep" we live *together* with Him. We are to comfort and edify each other, not live in a fear of tribulation. Salvation is totally by grace and the meeting in the air comprises part of that salvation.

6 Therefore let us not sleep, as do others; but let us watch and be sober.
7 For they that sleep sleep in the night; and they that be drunken are drunken in the night.
8 But let us, who are of the day, be sober, putting on the breastplate of faith and love; and for an helmet, the hope of salvation.
9 For God hath not appointed us to wrath, but to obtain salvation by our Lord Jesus Christ,
10 Who died for us, that, whether we wake or sleep, we should live together with him.
11 Wherefore comfort yourselves together, and edify one another, even as also ye do. (1Thessalonians 5:6-11).

7. The world will be shocked and spiritually awakened by the absence of the Church.

Popular books and tapes promote the idea that the world will be so affected by the rapture that many will turn to the Lord. The Bible teaches the opposite.

8 And then shall that Wicked be revealed, whom the Lord
shall consume with the spirit of his mouth, and shall destroy
with the brightness of his coming:
9 Even him, whose coming is after the working of Satan
with all power and signs and lying wonders,
10 And with all deceivableness of unrighteousness in them
that perish; because they received not the love of the truth,
that they might be saved.
11 And for this cause God shall send them strong delusion,
that they should believe a lie:
12 That they all might be damned who believed not the
truth, but had pleasure in unrighteousness. (2 Thessalonians
2:8-12).

8. The purpose of the Judgment Seat of Christ is to see
    whether a person is worthy of entering Heaven.
    Salvation is totally by grace and is "no more of works"
"not by works" "not of works."

And if by grace, then is it no more of works: otherwise grace
is no more grace. But if it be of works, then is it no more
grace: otherwise work is no more work. (Romans 11:6).

8 For by grace are ye saved through faith; and that not of
yourselves: it is the gift of God: 9 Not of works, lest any
man should boast. (Ephesians 2:8-9).
Not by works of righteousness which we have done, but
according to his mercy he saved us, by the washing of
regeneration, and renewing of the Holy Ghost; (Titus 3:5).

9. The Judgment Seat of Christ is to deal with sins committed
    before or after salvation.
    All of our sins were paid for by Christ on the cross. Since
all of our sins were in the future when He died, how can
anyone say He only paid for a portion of them?

20 Moreover the law entered, that the offence might abound. But where sin abounded, grace did much more abound:
21 That as sin hath reigned unto death, even so might grace reign through righteousness unto eternal life by Jesus Christ our Lord. (Romans 5:20-21).

8 But God commendeth his love toward us, in that, while we were yet sinners, Christ died for us.
9 Much more then, being now justified by his blood, we shall be saved from wrath through him.
10 For if, when we were enemies, we were reconciled to God by the death of his Son, much more, being reconciled, we shall be saved by his life.
(Romans 5:8-10).

10. Unconfessed sins are dealt with at the Judgment Seat of Christ.

This is taught on the basis of 1 John 1:9. However, our forgiveness is not based upon confessing sins. 1 John is a book that does not deal (doctrinally) with the Church age. The believer in this age only confesses faith in Christ.

Nothing in the passages regarding the Judgment Seat of Christ indicate "sins" or "sin" is judged. One sin is enough to send a person to Hell. If we are forgiven on the basis of our confessing sins, salvation is works PLUS Christ, and is not by grace alone.

13 Every man's work shall be made manifest: for the day shall declare it, because it shall be revealed by fire; and the fire shall try every man's work of what sort it is.
14 If any man's work abide which he hath built thereupon, he shall receive a reward.
15 If any man's work shall be burned, he shall suffer loss: but he himself shall be saved; yet so as by fire. (1 Corinthians 3:13-15).

That if thou shalt confess with thy mouth the Lord Jesus, and shalt believe in thine heart that God hath raised him from the dead, thou shalt be saved. (Romans 10:9).

11. Believers living at the rapture must die before they go to Heaven.

This error is brought on by taking a general statement and making it a specific requirement. The passage used for this is:

And as it is appointed unto men once to die, but after this the judgment: (Hebrews 9:27).

However, the word of God says:

51 Behold, I shew you a mystery; We shall not all sleep, but we shall all be changed,
52 In a moment, in the twinkling of an eye, at the last trump: for the trumpet shall sound, and the dead shall be raised incorruptible, and we shall be changed. (1 Corinthians 15:51-52).

There are several examples in the Bible of men dying twice. (Lazarus, son of the widow in Luke 7, etc.) and some men not dying at all (Enoch).

By faith Enoch was translated that he should not see death; (Hebrews 11:5).

12. Only a preacher's or teacher's work is dealt with at the Judgment Seat of Christ.

The scripture makes it clear that all believers must stand before the Judgment Seat of Christ. Of course there will not be 2 or 3 separate Judgment Seats, which is another indication that the rapture includes the entire Body of Christ, not a split or partial rapture where some are caught out and some are left to go into the Tribulation.

For we must all appear before the judgment seat of Christ; that every one may receive the things done in his body, according to that he hath done, whether it be good or bad. (2 Corinthians 5:10).

Bible Passages Related to the Rapture.

13 But I would not have you to be ignorant, brethren, concerning them which are asleep, that ye sorrow not, even as others which have no hope.
14 For if we believe that Jesus died and rose again, even so them also which sleep in Jesus will God bring with him.
15 For this we say unto you by the word of the Lord, that we which are alive and remain unto the coming of the Lord shall not prevent them which are asleep.
16 For the Lord himself shall descend from heaven with a shout, with the voice of the archangel, and with the trump of God: and the dead in Christ shall rise first:
17 Then we which are alive and remain shall be caught up together with them in the clouds, to meet the Lord in the air: and so shall we ever be with the Lord.
18 Wherefore comfort one another with these words.
(1Thessalonians 4:13-18).

8 We are confident, I say, and willing rather to be absent from the body, and to be present with the Lord.
9 Wherefore we labour, that, whether present or absent, we may be accepted of him.
10 For we must all appear before the judgment seat of Christ; that every one may receive the things done in his body, according to that he hath done, whether it be good or bad.
11 Knowing therefore the terror of the Lord, we persuade men; but we are made manifest unto God; and I trust also are made manifest in your consciences.
(2 Corinthians 5:8-11).

10 According to the grace of God which is given unto me, as a wise masterbuilder, I have laid the foundation, and another buildeth thereon. But let every man take heed how he buildeth thereupon.
11 For other foundation can no man lay than that is laid, which is Jesus Christ.

12 Now if any man build upon this foundation gold, silver, precious stones, wood, hay, stubble;
13 Every man's work shall be made manifest: for the day shall declare it, because it shall be revealed by fire; and the fire shall try every man's work of what sort it is.
14 If any man's work abide which he hath built thereupon, he shall receive a reward.
15 If any man's work shall be burned, he shall suffer loss: but he himself shall be saved; yet so as by fire.
(1 Corinthians 3:10-15).

49 And as we have borne the image of the earthy, we shall also bear the image of the heavenly.
50 Now this I say, brethren, that flesh and blood cannot inherit the kingdom of God; neither doth corruption inherit incorruption.
51 Behold, I shew you a mystery; We shall not all sleep, but we shall all be changed,
52 In a moment, in the twinkling of an eye, at the last trump: for the trumpet shall sound, and the dead shall be raised incorruptible, and we shall be changed.
53 For this corruptible must put on incorruption, and this mortal must put on immortality. (1 Corinthians 15:49-53).

THE JUDGMENT SEAT OF CHRIST
(A Sermon Outline)

Every person is going to a judgment. If you are lost, upon death you are cast into Hell, for you have rejected God's offer of pardon and forgiveness through Christ. In the future you will be brought up out of Hell to stand before God's Great White Throne and hear the formal charges against you and the justification of them.

You will enter into the court guilty as charged and be cast into the lake of fire for all eternity.

If you are saved, you have a court date before the Judgment Seat of Christ where your WORK of this life will be tried. A reward is given for faithful service.

APPEARANCE NOTICE

8 We are confident, I say, and willing rather to be absent from the body, and to be present with the Lord.

9 Wherefore we labour, that, whether present or absent, we may be accepted of him.

10 For we must all appear before the judgment seat of Christ; that every one may receive the things done in his body, according to that he hath done, whether it be good or bad.

11 Knowing therefore the terror of the Lord, we persuade men; but we are made manifest unto God; and I trust also are made manifest in your consciences. (2 Corinthians 5:8-11).

ACCESS TO THE COURT

13 But I would not have you to be ignorant, brethren, concerning them which are asleep, that ye sorrow not, even as others which have no hope.

14 For if we believe that Jesus died and rose again, even so them also which sleep in Jesus will God bring with him.

15 For this we say unto you by the word of the Lord, that we which are alive and remain unto the coming of the Lord shall not prevent them which are asleep.

16 For the Lord himself shall descend from heaven with a shout, with the voice of the archangel, and with the trump of God: and the dead in Christ shall rise first:

17 Then we which are alive and remain shall be caught up together with them in the clouds, to meet the Lord in the air: and so shall we ever be with the Lord.

18 Wherefore comfort one another with these words. (1Thessalonians 4:13-18).

ACKNOWLEDGEMENT OF COURT DATE

49 And as we have borne the image of the earthy, we shall also bear the image of the heavenly.

50 Now this I say, brethren, that flesh and blood cannot inherit the kingdom of God; neither doth corruption inherit incorruption.
51 Behold, I shew you a mystery; We shall not all sleep, but we shall all be changed,
52 In a moment, in the twinkling of an eye, at the last trump: for the trumpet shall sound, and the dead shall be raised incorruptible, and we shall be changed.
53 For this corruptible must put on incorruption, and this mortal must put on immortality. (1 Corinthians 15:49-53).

ARRAIGNMENT OF HEARING

10 According to the grace of God which is given unto me, as a wise masterbuilder, I have laid the foundation, and another buildeth thereon. But let every man take heed how he buildeth thereupon.
11 For other foundation can no man lay than that is laid, which is Jesus Christ.
12 Now if any man build upon this foundation gold, silver, precious stones, wood, hay, stubble;
13 Every man's work shall be made manifest: for the day shall declare it, because it shall be revealed by fire; and the fire shall try every man's work of what sort it is.
14 If any man's work abide which he hath built thereupon, he shall receive a reward.
15 If any man's work shall be burned, he shall suffer loss: but he himself shall be saved; yet so as by fire.
(1 Corinthians 3:10-15).

TRIBULATION AND THE CHURCH

Will the church go through the tribulation? This question is debated by many. It is important because the church needs to know, and the answer depends on proper Bible interpretation, as well as an understanding of right division.
There are four views regarding the question.

1. Partial Rapture.
2. Post-tribulation Rapture.
3. Mid-tribulation Rapture.
4. Pre-tribulation Rapture.

We are Pretribulational Premillennialists. This means the Church is raptured before the tribulation, and the Lord Jesus Christ will return to earth after the Tribulation to set up the Millennial Kingdom. Our position is the fourth one, namely, the Church (body of Christ) will not be in any part of the Tribulation period. The entire body of Christ will be raptured prior to any portion of the Tribulation. We will examine each view and give the scriptural reasons for rejecting the first three views and accepting the fourth view.

PARTIAL RAPTURE

The Partial Rapture view is currently very popular, especially among groups that emphasize works. Since it is, in their view, the particular behavior of the believer that determines whether or not he is caught out before the Tribulation, any deviation from the group's arbitrary set of standards decides whether or not he goes into part or all of the Tribulation. The doctrine also opens the door for people saved during the Tribulation to be a part of the body of Christ. A popular set of books (designed to be read by those who are novices in Bible doctrine) has various titles such as "Left Behind," etc. This series appeals to the natural man because there are fabricated scenarios and a hint of a "second chance" to accept the Lord in the Tribulation.
The key to getting raptured prior to the Tribulation, according to this view, is to be obedient or to have a "second work of grace" (sometimes identified as a Holy Ghost baptism or some special appearance from God) that sets you apart from other believers. They teach that the obedient group will be raptured before the Tribulation, while the remainder of believers goes into the tribulation to learn and repent of their prior disobedience. It is almost a type of Protestant purgatory.

The emphasis of this view is on the <u>behavior</u> of the believer. Some deliberate sin or lack of an experience determines the rupture. There are a few who attempt to make it simply a Bible determination, having nothing to do with the prior behavior of the church, but they are a minority.

In other words, the Partial Rapture theory is not based upon prophetic promises, general church apostasy, or world events, it is entirely up to the individual. Whereas the Mid-trib and Post-trib views stress the need for the entire church to be cleansed from its apostasy, or purged for ungodliness, the Partial Rapture concentrates on the individual scare of not being ready.

POST-TRIBULATION RAPTURE

Post-tribulationists concentrate on passages that warn of general tribulation for believers. The word, tribulation, is used in a technical prophetic sense as well as in a non-technical and non-prophetic sense in the Bible. There are warnings that believers can suffer "tribulation" during various times, but "the time of Jacob's trouble" is not the same as day by day tribulations. Paul gives both usages, technical and non-technical, in the following passage.

4 So that we ourselves glory in you in the churches of God for your patience and faith in all your persecutions and tribulations that ye endure:
5 Which is a manifest token of the righteous judgment of God, that ye may be counted worthy of the kingdom of God, for which ye also suffer:
6 Seeing it is a righteous thing with God to recompense tribulation to them that trouble you;
7 And to you who are troubled rest with us, when the Lord Jesus shall be revealed from heaven with his mighty angels,
8 In flaming fire taking vengeance on them that know not God, and that obey not the gospel of our Lord Jesus Christ:
9 Who shall be punished with everlasting destruction from the presence of the Lord, and from the glory of his power;

(2 Thessalonians 1:4-9)

2 By whom also we have access by faith into this grace wherein we stand, and rejoice in hope of the glory of God.
3 And not only so, but we glory in tribulations also: knowing that tribulation worketh patience;
4 And patience, experience; and experience, hope:
5 And hope maketh not ashamed; because the love of God is shed abroad in our hearts by the Holy Ghost which is given unto us. (Romans 5:2-5)

Almost every saint can claim "tribulations" (2 Thessalonians 1:4 and Romans 5:3) during his life, some more than others. The "tribulation" (singular in 2 Thessalonians 1:6) is not day by day trouble of the believer; this Tribulation is experienced by those who are enemies of God. But regardless of where it is found, almost any mention of the word "tribulation" is synonymous, in the Post-Tribulation Rapturist's view, with the future time of Tribulation. They believe the entire church will go through the seven years of Tribulation, experiencing a cleansing and purging. This is to make the church ready to meet the Lord just prior to the Millennial Kingdom.

Two specific passages used by Post-tribulationists are the following:

33 These things I have spoken unto you, that in me ye might have peace. In the world ye shall have tribulation: but be of good cheer; I have overcome the world. (John 16:33)

22 Confirming the souls of the disciples, and exhorting them to continue in the faith, and that we must through much tribulation enter into the kingdom of God. (Acts 14:22)

It is important to notice that both passages indicate "tribulation" is one of a general sense. At the least, all should agree that both passages **could** refer to the trials of life experienced by many people.

"In the world ye shall have tribulation" is followed by an exhortation to be "of good cheer" — not a warning to correct their life so as to miss tribulation. Nor is there any reference in either passage to connect the idea of tribulation with a prophetic judgment.

One major passage the Post-Tribulation view misappropriates is Matthew 24:1-14.

1 And Jesus went out, and departed from the temple: and his disciples came to him for to shew him the buildings of the temple.
2 And Jesus said unto them, See ye not all these things? verily I say unto you, There shall not be left here one stone upon another, that shall not be thrown down.
3 And as he sat upon the mount of Olives, the disciples came unto him privately, saying, Tell us, when shall these things be? and what shall be the sign of thy coming, and of the end of the world?

The question and answer has to do with the time of the destruction of the temple and the sign of His coming and the end of the world. Noticing where they are (on the Mount of Olives) and who (Jewish disciples who know nothing of the reason for His coming death and the following Church Age) is asking the question go a long ways toward understanding the passage.

The Post-Tribulationist assumes the passage is directed to the Body of Christ, but the Body of Christ is not even in existence until at least after the resurrection. The Lord is answering the question in view of the dealing Of God with Israel and the nations during the tribulation period. He is not giving the events of the Church Age or catching out of the Church.

4 And Jesus answered and said unto them, Take heed that no man deceive you.

5 For many shall come in my name, saying, I am Christ; and shall deceive many.
6 And ye shall hear of wars and rumours of wars: see that ye be not troubled: for all these things must come to pass, but the end is not yet.
7 For nation shall rise against nation, and kingdom against kingdom: and there shall be famines, and pestilences, and earthquakes, in divers places.
8 All these are the beginning of sorrows.
9 Then shall they deliver you up to be afflicted, and shall kill you: and ye shall be hated of all nations for my name's sake.

Israel will be hated during the Tribulation with an intensity they have never experienced before. The "ye" of verse 9 is a particular nation in contrast to the "nations." It is not a contrast of "Church" versus the nations.

10 And then shall many be offended, and shall betray one another, and shall hate one another.
11 And many false prophets shall rise, and shall deceive many.
12 And because iniquity shall abound, the love of many shall wax cold.

Even within Israel there will be division and confusion because of the rise of the Antichrist who will deceive the nation into a brief covenant.

13 But he that shall endure unto the end, the same shall be saved.

This is a "faith that works" (James 2:20) situation; it is not the imputed righteousness based on the "faith of Jesus Christ" (Romans 3:21) as is the case during the Church Age. If this is Church Age doctrine, then salvation by grace "not of works" (Ephesians 2:8-9) is a lie.

It is not enduring to "the end of your life" as a faithful Christian. Neither is it enduring to the end of the Tribulation and being physically saved; that is understood and would be useless repetition if the Lord meant that. It goes without saying that if a man is alive after the Tribulation, he will still be alive.

This is a case where people keep their love for the Lord and each other, endure offenses and deception while rejecting iniquity and false prophets.

14 And this gospel of the kingdom shall be preached in all the world for a witness unto all nations; and then shall the end come.
(Matthew 24:1-14).

In this Age of Grace we are never told to preach the "gospel of the Kingdom." Paul does not use the term one time in thirteen books.
He calls the gospel we preach:
the gospel of God. (Romans 1:1).
the gospel of his Son. (Romans 1:9).
the gospel of Christ. (Romans 1:16).
the gospel of peace. (Romans 10:15).
the gospel of the uncircumcision. (Galatians 2:7).
the gospel of your salvation. (Ephesians 1:13).
the gospel of our Lord Jesus Christ. (2 Thessalonians 1:8).
my gospel. (2 Timothy 2:8).

Not one time are we told the "gospel of the Kingdom" has anything to do with this present Church Age. Not one time does Paul ever hint that this age will come to an end when we carry the gospel of the Kingdom to all nations.

In fact, during Paul's ministry the gospel of our Lord Jesus Christ went to every creature:

If ye continue in the faith grounded and settled, and be not moved away from the hope of the gospel, which ye have heard, and which was preached to every creature which is under heaven; whereof I Paul am made a minister; (Colossians 1:23).

The gospel we preach went to all nations during the first century:

25 Now to him that is of power to stablish you according to my gospel, and the preaching of Jesus Christ, according to the revelation of the mystery, which was kept secret since the world began,

26 But now is made manifest, and by the scriptures of the prophets, according to the commandment of the everlasting God, made known to all nations for the obedience of faith: (Romans 16:25-26).

During the first century after the death of Christ, the gospel of Grace went into all the world:

5 For the hope which is laid up for you in heaven, whereof ye heard before in the word of the truth of the gospel;

6 Which is come unto you, as it is in all the world; and bringeth forth fruit, as it doth also in you, since the day ye heard of it, and knew the grace of God in truth: (Colossians 1:5-6).

Regardless of how we define the terms: every creature, all nations, all the world; the Bible plainly states the gospel of the grace of God went to each one.

Justin Martyr (110-165) said this:
"There is no people, Greek or Barbarian or any other race by whatsoever appellation or manner they may be distinguished, however ignorant of art and agriculture, whether they dwell in tents or wander about in covered wagons, among who prayers and thanksgivings are not offered, in the name of the crucified Jesus, to the Father and creator of all things."[3]

---

[3] Robert Hall Glover, <u>The Progress of World-Wide Missions</u>, p. 21.

If the gospel Paul preached is the same as the gospel in Matthew 24, the question is, "Why did the end not come as promised by the Lord?"

The end did not come because the gospel of the Kingdom is not the same as the gospel we preach.

That gospel preached by the twelve and the early group of Acts believers was rejected by the nation of Israel. The culmination of their unbelief reached its height when they stoned Stephen in Acts 7, a man "full of faith and power" (Acts 6:8) and "full of the Holy Ghost." (Acts 7:55). The gospel of the Kingdom (King's Dominion) was withdrawn from Israel until the "Time of Jacob's Trouble" (Great Tribulation) brings her to her knees to call upon God.

God called another apostle and gave him the revelation of the present Church Age. Our gospel went into all the world in the first century due to the dedication of those believers to our task. After the first century, the "last days" (2 Timothy 3:1-13) of the Church Age began, and a "falling away" (2 Thessalonians 5:2) has been the order of the day ever since. Each generation of the Church Age carries us farther from doing what the Lord told us to do in this age: world evangelization. The Church has more today and does less than each preceding generation. We build ten churches on Main Street USA, while 300 million have never heard the Name of Jesus one time.

Even if we carried the gospel to all in our generation, we have no promise the Lord will come to catch the Church out because of our obedience. The Church has no signs; we have only Scripture, and that is sufficient to "throughly" furnish us unto all good works. (2 Timothy 3:16-17).

The gospel of the Kingdom will be preached in the future Tribulation period.

That preaching is headed by angels, (Revelation 10:5-6;11:15;14:6-7) two witnesses who are martyred and resurrected on CNN, (Revelation 11) and 144,000 male Jewish virgins, (Revelation 7,14) with the gift of languages (tongues) and signs of the Kingdom, totally dedicated to get the gospel out to the world. They do it in less than seven years. (Revelation 7:9). Then, THE END comes.

The Post-tribulation view emphasizes the general idea that all of the church must go through the Tribulation period simply because no promises are given to exclude the church from it, or the church needs some cleansing from its apostasy before meeting the Lord. The Post-Tribulation Rapture view also fails to rightly divide the Bible by confusing Tribulation doctrine with Church Age doctrine: Israel's responsibilities, promises and judgment, with those pertaining to the Body of Christ.

MID-TRIBULATION RAPTURE

The Mid-Tribulation Rapture view says the church will go through part of the tribulation (usually 3 ½ years) and then will be raptured before the beginning of the second half. Since the term "church" is used in the book of Revelation, and there are *some* churches associated, in their view, with first half events of the tribulation in the book, they conclude there is a mid-tribulational rapture of the church.

Of course the Mid-Tribulationist twists, changes, goes to the Greek, or wherever to prove the Book of Revelation churches are in the Church Age. The problem is simply one of believing the Bible.

John writes from a position of being in the "Lord's Day." (Revelation 1:10). As Ezekiel was transported in time over to the Millennium to see the rebuilt temple, John was moved to the Lord's Day (a day of darkness and judgment. Amos 5:20) and saw *Tribulation churches*, not the Church which is the Body of Christ.

These churches have angels over them (Revelation 2-3). _The_ Greek says what? Is that the _inspired original_ you are quoting? If you don't believe the book you are quoting is the inspired word of God, we have no time to answer your questions about "angellos." Your problem is one Greek definitions can not fix. These churches are not "members of his body, of his flesh, and of his bones" (Ephesians 5:30) as we are — they can be spit out of His mouth. (Revelation 3:16). And, to make matters worse, if they don't overcome, they will be cast into the lake of fire. (Revelation 2:11). Those who do overcome will eat of the tree of life (Revelation 2:7). At this point, the child of God who knows he is a member of the Body of Christ already (Ephesians 5:30) and unable to be separated from Christ (Romans 8:38-39) with the promise of a glorified body (Philippians 3:21) that does not need a tree of life, should begin to see something is different.

The Mid-Tribulationist does the same thing as the Post-Tribulationist; he does not know the difference between Israel and the Body of Christ.

There are wars and pestilences in the first half, but before what they see as "wrath" poured out upon the inhabitants of the earth, their Mid-Tribulation church will be raptured out of it. The view is an attempt to answer the Partial-Rapture and Post-Tribulation Rapture points, but still associates the church with some aspect of the Tribulation.

PRE-TRIBULATION RAPTURE

All of the above views fail in three critical areas. The Pre-tribulation Rapture is the only view that follows these rules:
1. Believe the Bible.
2. Rightly Divide the Bible.

3. Recognize Paul's unique ministry as the "apostle of the Gentiles."

1 Thessalonians: "caught up"

In the Epistle to the Thessalonians we are reminded again and again of the imminent coming of the Lord Jesus. In the first chapter of the epistle we read, **"Ye turned to God from idols to serve the living and true God, and to wait for His Son from heaven." (1 Thessalonians 1:10 KJB)** There are seven references to the coming of the Lord Jesus Christ in this First Epistle to the Thessalonians alone.

In relation to the coming of the Lord Jesus. We are told that "we shall be caught up together to meet the Lord in the air." It was these words, "caught up," that arrested my attention (4:17)

This word that we have here translated "caught up" is a very forcible one in English and Greek. The reference to "serve and waiting" (1:10) was to the first century Thessalonica church, it is quite different 20 centuries later (today).

Greek is not necessary to understanding the word of God—but proper use and knowledge of the Greek Textus Receptus (from which the KJB NT was translated) to supplement the English of the KJB is permissible. The English word "catch" is defined in the Oxford English Dictionary (OED) as:

"to seize or capture, especially after pursuit: *to catch a criminal; to catch a runaway horse.*

to trap or ensnare: *to catch a fish.*"

Used as an adjective "caught up": "To be involved involuntarily."

(Sadly, many so-called "Greek experts" do not know how up to date and accurate the 'old archaic English' terms are!)

The Greek word harpazo, translated "caught up," means to take away by force, as when a wild beast seizes and carries off its prey, or as when one snatches a thing from another.

We might also add that the English phrase "caught up" may imply the same meaning as the Greek term "harpazo" or unlike Greek, apart from scripture, in secular use have even more meanings. Proper Greek (or any language) usage in Bible study never corrects the word of God, but serves to enhance KJB English understanding and study.

It is of interest to notice where the same Greek word occurs in the New Testament. In Matthew 11:12 it is "take by force," in speaking of the violent taking the kingdom of heaven. In John 6:15 the same term is given, "take by force," where reference is made to the Jews, who would make Christ a King. In John 10:12 the word is given "catcheth," in speaking of the wolf catching the sheep, through the cowardice of the hireling shepherd. Acts 8:39 the word is translated "caught away," in speaking of Philip being caught away by the Holy Spirit after he had been speaking to the eunuch. Twice the word is translated "caught up" in 2 Corinthians 12:2-4, in referring to the apostle being caught up to the third heaven. Revelation 12:5 the term is rendered "caught up."

From all these references we see at once the forcible meaning of the word, which means "to snatch away." When the Lord Jesus Christ comes for His own, we read that He is going to snatch us away and take us to Himself.

It is true that the term "rapture" is found nowhere in the KJB. But that does not mean that "rapture" when correctly used is a *false Biblical doctrine.* Like the term "Trinity", a term also not found in scripture; both terms combine a group of scripture words or doctrines to describe in one word a true Biblical doctrine. It is always best to stay with scripture words but I understand the use of terms to describe theological doctrines. "Rapture" can imply not only a forcible catching out of one situation, but it also is to be effectually placed into a much more joyous and blessed experience. In the same way, the term "Trinity" combines many Bible references to Three Persons, all with the same Divine Attributes, working in Divine harmony of the Godhead: "Tri—"(3 Persons) "—unity"(One God). In the One Godhead there are 3 equal Persons.

Acts_17:29 Forasmuch then as we are the offspring of God,*(Man is body, soul, and spirit in one person)* **we ought not to think that the Godhead is like unto gold, or silver, or stone, graven by art and man's device.**

Romans_1:20 For the invisible things of him from the creation of the world are clearly seen, being understood by the things that are made, even his eternal power and Godhead; so that they are without excuse: *(all people know there is a God — as well as Persons in the Godhead)*

Colossians_2:9 For in him dwelleth all the fulness of the Godhead bodily. *(All the Attributes of the Father and the Holy Spirit also dwell in Jesus Christ.)*

Why is the KJB reading "caught up" so important?

Why does the KJB not translate ἁρπάζω (harpazo) as "rapture"? "Rapture" in contemporary usage implies a joyous or enjoyable event: "A state, condition, or fit of intense delight or enthusiasm.' (OED). A "rapture" meaning "to seize" (as stated above) is obsolete! How is it that the KJB (supposedly archaic) is so up-to-date with "caught up", a word that means — *to take away by force, as when a wild beast seizes and carries off its prey, or as when one snatches a thing from another??* Or, why not the mild "taken up" (1 Thess 4:17) of the Common English Version?

The answer lies in understanding something about "right division" of the Bible. There are 7 economies, dispensations, or periods in God's dealing with His creation. Each economy has certain peculiar, individual, divine requirements; each period has certain requirements that are alike all others. Right division is the attempt to discover each. The seven economies are: Innocence, Conscience,

Government, Patriarchs, Law, Grace, and Kingdom. The KJB is laid out with corresponding chapters and books. For example: Innocence is found from Genesis 1-3, Conscience from Genesis 4-8, Government from Genesis 9-11, Patriarchs from Genesis 12-Exodus 19, Law from Exodus 19-Acts, Grace from Acts-Philemon, Kingdom from Hebrews-Revelation. EVERY dispensation or economy ended in apostasy from God's divine requirements and ended in judgment, from Genesis Innocence to the Law. The future end of Grace and the Kingdom is prophesied in the KJB to end the same way!

"Every day, in every way, we are getting better and better" is the pipedream of idiots. Every form of government run by man has failed and will fail. The perfect Government is yet to come—and it will not be anything materialistic.

Like Israel did under the Law dispensation, so will the age of Grace go. Israel ignored mercy and added strict ordinances which God never intended. The Feasts of the Lord became "the Jews Feasts". Mercy was overcome by tyranny and love overcome by hate.

The age or dispensation of Grace will not end in a joyous fit of anticipation. We have already proven that. The obedience of the "church" to the Lord's directions for this present age have already been like a load of garbage. The church age is characterized by grace—salvation not by works (Titus 3:5) no more of works (Romans 11:6) and the church has taken FULL advantage of that fact. Freedom from the Law has pushed licentiousness to the forefront. Anything goes. There are no restrictions; no boundaries, everything is good and accepted. There is no definite word of God and no Bible that is perfect. "Grace" abounds and heaven is silent. God allows man to have his day. This is the age of Grace and it ends in absolute disobedience and judgment.

That is why the body of Christ must be snatched out, unwillingly and unknowingly.

The doctrine of the catching out is defined:

I. SELECT AS TO THE INDIVIDUALS TAKEN.

Notice what the apostle says in v. 14, "For if we believe that Jesus died and rose again, even so them also which sleep in Jesus will God bring with Him." Here the apostle is not speaking to the world, but to Christians.

In the same way He speaks to the church at Corinth, when He says, "We shall not all sleep," etc. He is writing to those who are "saints." That is not a position we are to struggle to be in, but it is a position to which we are placed by God. A Christian is a saint, and as a saint he SHOULD do certain things; hence we are told do this or that, "as becometh saints."

The apostle in all the epistle is writing to *professing* Christians, and when he speaks of "If we believe," and "our gathering together unto Christ," common sense as well as Scripture will tell us that the Spirit of God is speaking of the fact that it is only believers who will be taken away when Christ comes again.

The last sight the world had of Christ was upon the cross. They said, "Away with Him, and crucify Him," and that is the end of Him as far as the world was concerned.

I believe every child of God will be caught away, for the whole argument is based upon, "If we believe that Jesus died and rose again," then certain consequences will ensue. We believe that Jesus died for our sins. We cannot be Christians without that basic belief.

II. SURE AS TO ITS OCCURRENCE.

The world says such and such a thing is as sure as death *and taxes* ; but a Christian should not speak in that manner, because the most unlikely thing for a Christian is to die. The rapture can occur at any moment — without sign or warning.

III. SECRET IN ITS METHOD.

There is a terrible time coming which is spoken of in the Old Testament as the "time of Jacob's trouble," and in the New Testament as "the great tribulation." We read of those who shall be saved out of it; for before that time, the Lord Jesus Christ comes for His body and takes them away. (Romans 5:9; 1 Thess 5:9)

IV. SUDDEN IN ITS OPERATION.

There are two Scriptures which specially speak of the suddenness of Christ's coming, one with reference to His coming as the Son of Man to the earth, and the other with reference to His coming to complete the redemption of those who believe in Him. In one of these passages the coming of Christ is likened in its suddenness to the lightning flashing across the sky, and the apostle tells us that we shall not all sleep, but we shall be changed, in the twinkling of an eye. In an atom of time, so small that it cannot be reckoned, it cannot be analyzed, this momentous change will take place. We may be at some meeting, or we may be in the pursuit of our ordinary daily occupation, when the change will come, and mortality will put on immortality.

1Cor 15:52 " In a moment, in the twinkling of an eye, at the last trump: for the trumpet shall sound, and the dead shall be raised incorruptible, and we shall be changed."

V. SAVING IN ITS ISSUE.

(Philippians 3:20-21 KJB) For our conversation is in heaven; from whence also we look for the Saviour, the Lord Jesus Christ:

21 Who shall change our vile body, that it may be fashioned like unto his glorious body, according to the working whereby he is able even to subdue all things unto himself.

To look for Him is good, to see Him is better, to be like Him is best, and better than the best is to be with Him, for that ensures all the rest.

VI. SATISFYING IN ITS OUTCOME.

It is Christ Himself that we long to see. Nothing else will satisfy our hearts. In studying prophecy do not let us forget or lose sight of Him as the central figure. We long to see Christ face to face, for when we see Him we shall be satisfied, and, more than that, He will be satisfied. **"The Lord direct your hearts into the love of God and into the patience of Christ,"** was Paul's word to the church at Thessalonica. What is the patience of Christ? The patience that Christ is exercising now in waiting till the Church is complete, and then He will come to take us to Himself. He will not be satisfied until His redeemed are with Him. And we with the Psalmist say, "I shall be satisfied when I awake in His likeness."

Most hymnals are filled with words about dying and going to Heaven. Very few mention the rapture of the body of Christ. Sermons are fewer on the IMMINENT rapture of the body of Christ as the ages roll on. Why?

I believe there are at least two reasons:

1. It has been about 19 centuries since the promise was made. In the first century Paul commended the church at Thessalonica for "waiting on the coming of the Lord" while they worked for Him. The length of time has dulled the church expectation — but the promise has not been rescinded.

2. The general apostasy of "Which Bible?" has removed the force of the next IMMINENT event on God's timetable. Many Christians don't know where the inerrant, infallible word of God is! How can there be eager anticipation of a Bible event when the promise is questioned?